"Harvey Mackay is one of the greatest writers of our time. And *Sharkproof* is the best of the great books Harvey has written. It possesses all the qualities of a winner and is surely another best-seller by this popular author."
— NORMAN VINCENT PEALE

"You don't need an M.B.A. to enjoy and profit from Harvey's rapid-fire delivery of motivation, inspiration, and common sense about today's radically changed employment environment."
— PRESTON TOWNLEY,
President & Chief Executive Officer,
The Conference Board

"This is Harvey Mackay's latest and his best. I think it will break all records. Harvey loves to write and he is good at it."
— WALTER F. MONDALE,
Former Vice President of the United States

"A mother lode of timely, hard-earned, bite-sized, street-smart golden nuggets. Harvey's opening completely surprised me and doubly credibilized the rest. Invaluable for job seekers, employed or unemployed."
—STEPHEN R. COVEY,
Author of *The Seven Habits of Highly Effective People* and *Principle-Centered Leadership*

"Harvey explodes up the middle with the kind of kick-butt motivation that will put your career in the win column. It's like watching next week's game film instead of last week's."

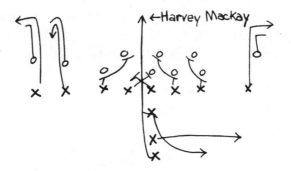

—DENNIS GREEN,
Head Coach,
Minnesota Vikings

"I am waiting for *Sharkproof* to hit the bookstores so I can send it to several unemployed friends who need the kind of advice Mackay so pungently gives."
—STANLEY MARCUS,
Chairman Emeritus,
Neiman-Marcus Marketing Consultant

"*Sharkproof* is a terrific resource for the workers of today who want to be entrepreneurs of tomorrow. Harvey Mackay's common sense ideas can help make the most of your creative abilities, aspirations, and potential."

—JACK KEMP,
Secretary of the United States
Department of Housing and Urban Development

"At last someone who knows what he's talking about when it comes to 'jobs, jobs, jobs.' Harvey Mackay is smart, concise and best of all—he's not running for anything."

—MARK RUSSELL,
Political Satirist

"You can't count on the big company to take care of you anymore, so you have to count on yourself. And *Sharkproof* is the witty self-help guide you need to get off the crumbling corporate ladder before it collapses."

—ROSABETH MOSS KANTER,
Professor,
Harvard Business School,
Coauthor of *The Challenge of Organizational Change*

"This is the right book, baby . . . uh huh."
—CRAIG WEATHERUP,
Chief Executive Officer,
Pepsi-Cola North America

"Harvey Mackay's book is more than a how-to book. It's a survival guide to the 90s. In today's uncertain job market, smart managers realize that everyone's job is vulnerable, and not to be prepared for the worst is just plain dumb. Witty, entertaining and insightful, *Sharkproof* is certainly a winner and a must-read."
—EARL GRAVES,
Publisher and Chief Executive Officer,
Black Enterprise magazine

"Harvey Mackay shares his passion for loving your work just as he lives it every day and, in the process, provides an invaluable set of tips for job seekers and job holders alike."
—WILLIAM W. GEORGE,
President and Chief Executive Officer,
Medtronic, Incorporated

"In this stunning book, Harvey Mackay displays a warm, witty and compassionate voice which the reader instantly trusts. Speaking straight from the heart, Mackay makes you feel as if you were listening to the advice of a wise and caring father. The book is a classic."

—DORIS KEARNS GOODWIN,
Historian and Biographer

"Stop, look, and listen intently to the sage advice of Harvey Mackay. This guy is a wizard when it comes to getting, keeping, and loving a career. *Sharkproof* shares the secrets."

—KEN DYCHTWALD, PH.D.,
Age Wave, Inc.

"Harvey Mackay has done it again. He taught us how to *Swim with the Sharks*. Now he gives us the insight on how not to be eaten alive. In his latest book, *Sharkproof,* he candidly recognizes the problems facing all of us in this ever changing world and gives us not only hope, but the tools to create our own successful future. Another winner by a winner."

—JOE THEISMANN,
Entrepreneur

"The timeliness of this guide both to securing and retaining jobs is excellent. Mackay's advice can be of enormous value, particularly to young college graduates seeking employment opportunities, as many of the major companies in the country are cutting back and limiting jobs. This book will head the urgent reading list."

—JOAB THOMAS,
President,
Penn State University

"Whether you are on the 50 yard line—or number 50 in the unemployment line, everyone, and I do mean everyone, will profit from the wise advice in *Sharkproof.* It's your passport to getting the job you want in the 90s."

—LOU HOLTZ,
Head Football Coach,
University of Notre Dame

"I read a lot of books about business. All too often these books are too academic, science fiction, or just self-promotion. But Harvey Mackay's *Sharkproof* is a standout. It's a uniquely useful and practical executive survival guide for the perilous 90s and it came not a minute too soon."

—RICHARD M. FERRY,
President & Chief Executive Officer
Korn/Ferry International

"This book by Harvey Mackay is a MUST for anyone who has a job, as well as those out of work. In my profession, many coaches lose their positions each year. It hurts and in most cases we are so visible, it is more difficult because everyone in the country knows about it. *Sharkproof* will not only help get us back in the work force, it will soften the blow and give us valuable tools to bounce back."

—DON JAMES,
Head Coach,
University of Washington

"Dive in! *Sharkproof* proves that it's safe to go in the water. Mackay's book is an equivalent to an M.B.A. in career planning. Buckle up because now you're in the driver's seat of your future."

—DENNIS KIMBRO,
Author of *Think & Grow Rich: A Black Choice*

"*Sharkproof* beats shark bait. Harvey Mackay shows us how to get and keep the job we want. The perfect handbook for the nineties."

—CARL SEWELL,
Author of *Customers for Life*

"A book full of wisdom, common sense, and insight. Well worth reading."
—MARIAN WRIGHT EDELMAN,
President and Founder,
Children's Defense Fund,
Author of *The Measure of Our Success*

"Harvey's done it again! A book written with grace, style, and filled with nuggets of wisdom, not just about getting and holding a job; although that's there in spades. Beyond that, *Sharkproof* is how we can live better lives, how we can cope and learn from adversity; it's about leading a full, happy, and productive life. 'This is the true joy in life,' as George Bernard Shaw said: 'the being used for a PURPOSE recognized by yourself as a mighty one.' That's what *Sharkproof* is all about: the true joy in life."
—WARREN BENNIS,
University Professor and Distinguished Professor of
Business Administration,
University of Southern California

"Harvey's first book was a touchdown.
The second was a homerun.
Sharkproof is a slam dunk."
—PAT O'BRIEN
CBS Television

SHARKPROOF

GET THE JOB YOU WANT, KEEP THE JOB YOU LOVE . . . IN TODAY'S FRENZIED JOB MARKET

HARVEY B. MACKAY

HarperBusiness
A Division of HarperCollins*Publishers*

Also by Harvey B. Mackay

SWIM WITH THE SHARKS WITHOUT BEING EATEN ALIVE

BEWARE THE NAKED MAN WHO OFFERS YOU HIS SHIRT

HarperCollins books may be purchased for educational, business, or sales promotional use. For information please write: Special Markets Department, HarperCollins Publishers, Inc., 10 East 53rd Street, New York, NY 10022.

FIRST EDITION

Library of Congress Cataloging-in-Publication Data

Mackay, Harvey.
   Sharkproof: get the job you want, keep the job you love . . . in today's frenzied job market / Harvey B. Mackay.—1st ed.
     p.   cm.
   Includes index.
   ISBN 0-88730-619-5
   1. Job hunting.   I. Title.
HF5382.7.M32 1993
650.14—dc20   92-53494

93 94 95 96 97 ❖/HC 10 9 8 7 6 5 4 3 2 1

DEDICATION

My wife is the personal embodiment of the expression, "She won't take no for an answer!" When she decided there was a need for a new book about getting and keeping a job, and that I was the one to write it, she didn't stop needling me until I agreed to tackle it.

Thank you, Carol Ann, for our thirty-two exciting and fulfilling years together, and for knowing me better than I know myself. You were right ... I did have a lot I wanted to say.

CONTENTS

ACKNOWLEDGMENTS

As always, there are a number of people who work behind the scenes to help a writer put together the best book he can write. In my case, I had the pleasure of working with some of the best. They include:

My sister, Margie Resnick, whose X-ray vision helped me put together a manuscript that can be read without X-ray vision. I don't know what I would do without her sound and sage advice.

Lynne Lancaster, who has worked with me in the past, was, as always, a treasured sounding board from whom I always hear the truth, and an invaluable critic-in-residence. She is the best.

Jonathon Lazear, my agent and friend, who has been

at my side through three books and six successful years.

Ron Beyma is one of those fountains of information that can astonish you. He's a walking dictionary and encyclopedia, and was extremely helpful in the creation of *Sharkproof.*

Michael Schwager, my publicist for the past two books, has unfailingly been in my corner—with wit and dedication.

Vickie Abrahamson whose alert antennae sense the trends and trade winds long before the name-brand pundits get the forecast. She's on my A-list.

Judy McElheney, my assistant, has been as valuable to me as my own right arm and has proved it in a hundred different ways.

Linda Ferraro has kept us all in good spirits, held down the fort, and helped me in a myriad of ways.

Bill Miller for his creative input when I need him.

Judy Olausen is indisputably one of the best, most respected photographers around. And I've loved working with her again.

And to all my new friends at HarperBusiness and HarperCollins, especially my very able editor, Ed Breslin (possibly the wittiest man in North America), Bill Shinker, Susan Moldow, Virginia Smith, Joseph Montebello, Steve Magnuson, Brenda Segal, Brenda Marsh, Karen Mender, Lisa Berkowitz, and Jennifer Flannery.

My fact-checker extraordinaire was Leslye Friedberg.

A special thanks to an early reader of this book in its first draft. Susan Halligan's words of wisdom kept my momentum going and her enthusiasm was indeed appreciated.

Harvey B. Mackay
Minneapolis, Minnesota
August 1992

FOREWORD

You probably never heard of a foreword being written by a person who's not famous and not a writer. But I am a guy who's been there. I was looking for a job in sales after thirteen successful years and spent six soul-searching, gut-wrenching, ego-grinding months trying to get my career back on track.

And I did it. (You'll read about my story later in the book.)

They asked me to write the foreword because this book is for people like me—people who are out of work and struggling to get hired so you can feel good again, and people who have a job now and want to keep it.

During my search I was lucky enough to meet

Harvey Mackay, I was persistent enough to read all of his books, and I was motivated enough to put his advice into action.

Was it easy? No way. Was I afraid I was going to fail? You bet. Did Harvey's ideas prove to me I wasn't helpless and get me back to work? Absolutely yes!

Here are some of the things in this book that could help you find the job you want or keep the job you love. How to:

- Keep your head after you get the ax
- Overcome feeling rejected and turn your negative feelings into positive
- Assess your skills and talents and where you want to go in your career
- Understand what companies look for in job candidates and how you can differentiate yourself from the pack
- Know the questions interviewers ask and how to answer them
- Negotiate your new salary or ask for a raise
- Be so valuable to your company that you'll keep your job when others are losing theirs
- Build a network now so you'll have support in place when you do look for work
- Keep perspective on what's really important in your life

When I need to make my next job change, I know it's not going to be easy. But I also know I have two things to help me on my journey: One, techniques that make me stand out from millions of other job seekers, and two, a coach who will help me believe in myself even when no one else does. That's what you can find in this book.

Just remember, I did it, and with a little help you can do it, too.

Steve Nichols
Minneapolis, Minnesota

I

SINK OR SWIM?

YOU CAN OWN YOUR OWN BUSINESS AND STILL GET FIRED

Last year, after thinking it could never happen to me, figuratively speaking, I was fired.

It was over a year ago, and I'm still bitter about it. It was February 1991 and Mackay Envelope was coming off a C- to C+ year financially. We were hit by both national and industry trends but still holding our own in a business where it was 1929 revisited. In recent years, 240 thriving envelope companies had dwindled to two hundred.

Though our profitability was not where I would have liked it to be, it was clear we were going to be survivors, and our competitive position was more solid than ever. After nineteen A to A+ years in a row, I felt that C+ or C-wasn't really too bad, considering. My bankers of twenty years didn't agree and, virtually without notice, threw me out.

Naïvely, because I had sat across the table from them on many of the civic boards on which I served, had basked in their attaboys for my community work, sent them more leads than I had given to my sales manager, and been a model customer without a single complaint in all that time, I felt I was immune to the morés of the marketplace. Not so. A decade of reckless lending to every con artist with a wheelbarrow who called himself a developer had left the banking industry in a panic. Overly loose practices had given way to overly tight ones. Mass firings. All perks and amenities vanished. Even the philodendrons on Executive Row had been sentenced to death, and the bank offices themselves had taken on the carefree ambience of foxholes on Iwo Jima.

Banks were no longer running their own affairs. The bank examiners were in the drivers' seats and they drove Plymouths, not Porsches.

I should have seen it coming, but I didn't.

Worse, I hadn't taken my own advice: Instead of spreading my business around, I'd given 100 percent of it to one bank. All my eggs were in one basket, and they cracked every one of them over my head. That always happened to the other guy, not to me. Well, it happened, followed by a cheery, "Don't let the door hit you on the way out, Mr. Mackay."

How does this apply to the job market?

Don't be blindsided. A corporation is a lousy thing to fall in love with, because it won't love you back. You're never in the comfort zone, no matter what you think your position is. Keep your resume locked, loaded, and ready to fire at all times, your networking working, and your eyes and ears open for clues of changes coming that could be hazardous to the health of your career.

Never stop looking out for number one. And keep an eye on number two, also. If your boss seems to be on shaky ground, if bits and pieces of your department are starting to disappear, it could mean your whole department is about to be grafted onto the rear of the unemployment line. Firings used to be done with surgical cleanliness. Now they're called restructurings, and they're done with a meat cleaver. It's not just one body at a time anymore. Serial killers are on the loose, hacking away at every corporate personnel roster in the land.

For the first time in history, it's happening in professional ranks, too. Middle-aged lawyers, your well-established Harvard Law School types, partners in major law firms, who were sure they had lifetime guarantees, are being let go. They thought that being skilled professionals was enough, but it isn't anymore. Their fellow partners are showing them the door, if they aren't rainmakers too, bringing in new business and goosing up revenues for the firm. If it can happen to them, it can happen to the rest of us.

I strongly suggest you stow this in your brain bank:

Be prepared. We may be on our way out of the national recession, but there is nowhere you can hide that's guaranteed earthquake-proof against your own personal recession. The day can come when you, too, step into your boss's or your banker's office some Friday afternoon and hear, "I'm sorry to have to tell you this, but ..." It's not going to be easy, no matter how well prepared you are. But it's going to be a lot harder if you're like the 90 percent of us who aren't prepared when the bomb falls.

And it can happen to anyone, anytime.

2

SHARKBAIT: I GET FIRED A SECOND TIME IN THE SAME YEAR

When one area of my life goes sour I have the tendency to compensate in another area. Snooty bankers matter a lot less at the end of my seven-mile run than at the beginning.

It's hardly a novel approach. The first thing an executive outplacement service often does with its clients is to send them for a physical exam and, if they're able to handle it, cajole them into a fairly rigorous workout program.

You'll find the same advice in every book about job hunting, and all it will cost you is the price of a pair of sneakers.

You say you didn't have time to keep in shape when you were logging those twelve to fourteen hour days at National Widget? Well, friend, now you have plenty of time. And once you get rolling, you not only start to feel better physically, you also feel better emotionally.

Getting stronger and healthier helps put a lot of other things in perspective. You may have loved your job, but dying for love, particularly for love of a corporation, may not have been the smartest thing you ever did.

Once you feel the young tiger inside you start to stir again after years of slumber, it's a lot easier to handle the bumps in your career. And when you do go in for interviews, if you're in shape, you'll look better and have more self-confidence than you've had in years.

And so it was with me. My banker may have fired me, business may not have been the greatest, but all was not lost. In October and November of 1991, I ran back-to-back marathons in New York and the Twin Cities. At the time, it seemed like the most demanding physical challenge I'd ever set for myself. But because I had trained hard for the better part of four months, ratcheting up from my usual seven miles a day to even greater distances, it turned out to be much easier than I had expected. There I was, in top shape at age fifty-nine, both mentally and physically, happily married thirty-one years, three happy, well-adjusted kids, Mackay Envelope chugging along, banker or no, and though my pride had sustained a kind of fender bender, I really didn't have a care in the world.

Time for my annual physical checkup.

On December 12, my checkup reveals a slight chance I may have cancer of the prostate. In my mind it was 100-1 odds against. After all, fifty-nine-year-old guys who run two marathons in three weeks are obviously immortal. On Friday, December 13, I have a biopsy and my doctor tells me he is definitely concerned. The odds have dropped.

I tell my family members, my rabbi, and a few close friends. Results due Monday afternoon, 1:00 P.M.

I now digress for a moment to tell you that if the world were ordered according to my specifications, the first thing I would change is the Iron Rule of Health Care: "Nothing moves from Friday afternoon to Monday morning." Even the post office thinks that getting your Publishers Clearing House Sweepstakes entry form to you A.S.A.P. is important enough to give you Saturday service. But in the field of medicine, nothing short of multiple gunshot wounds is important enough to merit attention during that sacred sixty-five-hour stretch of medical downtime. As so many of you know who have had to go through similar experiences, unless it's a medical crisis for a loved one, life has no wringer to put you through to match this sucker.

At 1:12 P.M. on Monday, the phone rings and the three most dreaded words in the English language ring out loud and clear from Doctor Lundblad, "You have cancer." No human being is prepared for that experience.

The feeling is devastating. I had been handed my second pink slip in a year.

There had been positively no signal, no indication, no warning.

I felt like this time I had been fired from life. It was up to me to try to get rehired again.

3

HOW DO YOU KEEP YOUR HEAD AFTER YOU GET THE AX?

If you have immediate problems, as I did medically, you want the best possible advice and all of it you can get.

If you've just been fired from your job, the scenario isn't all that different.

Get help.

Get stabilized.

Get busy.

Whatever expert advice or help you need, you get. This is one you don't try to macho out on your own. As soon as the ax falls, negotiate your departure. They say they didn't want to fire you? Okay, let's work that guilty conscience to the max. Whatever is being offered, make sure it's fair. More severance. Reimbursement for unused vacation time and sick leave. Outplacement services. Office space. Office supplies. Secretarial help. Tuition.

Are they getting tough? You get tough. Hire a lawyer. In case you consider this advice anti-management, remember that no management bigwigs let themselves get fired without hiring the best legal advice they can.

Government assistance for the unemployed? Why not? You've been paying for it all these years. This is why.

Friends. Relatives. Old schoolmates. Customers. Vendors. Business associates. Professional advisers. Start leaning. Sad to say, they are not quite as interested in hearing about your troubles as you would like them to be. Ever see a live horse hanging around a dead horse? If you have, you won't see it for very long. Once the live one gets wind of his dead counterpart, he's gone. No mammal likes to linger in the presence of death. They leave as soon as decently possible. The exception is your faithful dog. He'll stick around and howl over your supine form. For a while. Until dinnertime, anyway.

Get help with the negative, but focus on the positive. You have something to offer. By helping you, all of the people whose assistance you solicit are helping themselves as well. They're helping put you back in a position where you can do them some good. They're piling up points against the time they may need the same kind of help.

You need to know where you stand and where you're going. You need to take inventory: financial, professional, and emotional. It's time to revise your budget. There are advisers who will tell you to cut down on everything. Not me. You can't cut down on your medical needs. If you can swing it, don't cut down on your kids' needs, even discretionary spending on their behalf. It hurts them too much;

they can't hide the hurt; you'll be infected by guilt that you can't hide; and that guilt will affect your own self-confidence and ability to perform. Borrow if you have to, but borrowing from yourself is best. Is your mortgage paid off? If interest rates are low, now's as good a time as any to refinance. Or take out a second mortgage.

What about Mom and Dad? Isn't this what moms and dads are for? Can they help you in starting your own business or in going back to school?

Or take your rich Uncle Fudd out to lunch. You always wondered why fate has given you so many relatives. Here's why. It's harder for them to say no, just as it is harder for them to squeeze you. Everyone in this country owes money. Now you owe your relatives. They can handle it. So can you. It's *why* you borrow that's going to make it easier on both of you. Americans are pretty good about paying for the education of others. We believe in education as a kind of capital improvement in the structure of society. It's a good investment. Don't be ashamed to borrow, particularly to replenish your professional inventory.

In fact, self-improvement is the one area in which you should really increase your spending, not decrease it.

Take courses. Upgrade your skills. You cannot ever afford to rest on the skills you learned in high school or college. The workplace is filling up with people who graduated long after you did and who have acquired newer, more efficient skills, who are young, who are eager and hungry to show those skills to your employer, and who don't care if they move you on down the road. Keep on going to school. Enhance what you already know and pick up new material. Computers. Language. Public speaking. Writing. Continuing education.

Nothing impresses me more as a potential employer than someone who is out of work but still actively going to school. In fact, what excuse is there for not being in a school of some kind when you're not employed? It's the true test of your determination to get into the workplace, to present an up-to-the-minute, trainable, quality package to a potential employer.

If you were fired, it's a great way to prove to yourself and others that you're capable of bouncing back after a setback. It's a real confidence builder.

It's the best single thing you can do for yourself.

Get stabilized. According to the Bureau of Labor Statistics, you're going to face 10.3 job changes in the course of a lifetime. Employment experts predict by the year 2000, the average worker will undergo five *career* changes.

Get a routine. Like yourself again. Make love to your wife, husband, boyfriend, girlfriend, or significant other. (Please select only one from the above list.) Spend some extra time with the kids. Read. Have a little fun.

Get busy. None of us have time to sit around feeling sorry for ourselves.

There are worse things than not working.

Just don't remind me again of what they are.

You also may be wondering at this point if I'm still around. The answer is a definite yes! It's been over a year since my prostate surgery, and I really feel great. I know you didn't buy this book to read all about my medical problems, but it figures that if you're defunct, so are your employment prospects. So if you're a male aged fifty or older, or have a loved one who is, Appendix C is required reading at this point. Otherwise let's move on to the next chapter, and get you that job.

4

WHY IS IT DIFFERENT THIS TIME?

Remember the good old days? Blue skies forever. All the cocktail party chatter was about soaring real estate values. The only things rising faster were salaries and bonuses. Suddenly, there's a warning shot across the bow. The crash of 1987. Not to worry. The economy takes a quick dip, then soars again. Within a few months the market is advancing again. You're back to the world of second homes. Third cars. Private schools. Season tickets. Fat farms. Cosmetic surgery.

And then, another economic sinking spell, but this time, there's no rebound. The recession rolls in. Takes hold. Sinks in. Bites down. Hard. We've had downturns before, but this one is different. This time it doesn't just hit the assembly line worker, the last-to-be-hired, first-to-be-fired minorities, and the marginal producers. This time it's the baby boomers, the middle managers, and the set-for-lifers who get it. Two million white-collar positions have been permanently eliminated. Millions more have been shrunk in terms of future prospects and growth. This time it isn't the other guy.

This time, it isn't only the first day of the rest of your life. It's the last day of your present job.

This time, it's you.

According to the Bureau of Labor Statistics, 40 percent of the people who lost their jobs in the recent recession were white-collar workers. In the 1982 slump, it was 20 percent.

The age of yuppies is over. The "dinks" ... double income, no kids ... have given way to the "dumpies" ... downwardly mobile professionals. According to David Letterman, the development of the self-firing executive isn't far off.

Now, it's posted notices on company bulletin boards. Restructuring and downsizing. Salary freezes. Bonuses canceled. Dreaded Friday afternoon calls to step down the hall and see the boss. The ax falls. Goodbye to the good times.

Naturally, there are no savings to speak of. Cash is trash. Why save at 7 percent, 8 percent, when real estate prices were rising at twice that rate and salaries three times as fast? When there were so many places to see? So much to buy?

The shoe starts to pinch. Cut back on the luxuries. Sure, but what about the obligations?

Traditionally, during recessions, the job squeeze grips tightest on the too young and the too old. Their financial responsibilities are mostly to themselves. Either they're just starting out with few major expenses or they're winding down, mortgage paid, retirement kitty ready to kick in and kids already grown and out on their own.

But this recession makes no concession to tradition. The people getting squeezed worst are 'tweeners: the people in their late twenties, thirties, forties, and early fifties, the middle managers in the middle years of their careers, still with kids to educate, mortgages to pay, retirements to fund, and elderly parents to care for. Bureau of Labor Statistics figures show that during the 1971–72 recession, just 40 percent of the unemployed were between twenty-five and fifty-four years old. By 1992, that figure had jumped to 63 percent.

There are also a few costly new wrinkles to contend with, like kids coming back to the nest after college or after the failure of their first marriages, and parents, who, as a result of advances in medical care, are more likely to live years longer than previous generations, and who may require long-term financial assistance.

The yawning gap between expectations and reality sets in. We begin to realize we can no longer expect the best of everything. Things aren't always going to get better.

The high salaries that have supported high lifestyles are the easy targets of companies having to contend with the emergent global economy. And the higher the salary, the easier the target.

The bumper sticker version of this sad situation can be seen posted on factory walls: "Those who are paid the least will be fired last." Companies can't worry about employees with high salaries when they've got those Japanese and Germans to compete against. Sayonara and auf Weidersehen, baby. The era of entitlement is over.

According to executive recruiter Charles Grevious,

"The truth of the matter is, job security is a thing of the past. The only thing you can do now is work on *employability security* ... building the right skills and learning to market yourself aggressively."

So, what happens next?

5

IF YOU REACH FOR THE STARS, AT LEAST YOU'LL GET OFF THE GROUND

Most important of all, you *will* survive.

Despite the gloomy picture just painted here, trends have occurred that make some aspects of the economic situation better, not worse, for employees and job seekers.

1. There used to be a little piece of folk wisdom: "The good people are all working." It's not true anymore. There have been just too many layoffs of too many good people in recent years. There's no longer any stigma attached to being laid off. It's a fact of business life today.

2. Since the 1960s, the social revolution has transformed the traditional Ozzie and Harriet American family

into a two-income household. Okay, so you're out of work. Well, your spouse probably isn't. Not great, but still a lot better than it was when there was only one bread-winner in the family. No spouse? No stigma there either. Alternative lifestyles are in. Tune in Monday night for the next episode of "Murphy Brown."

3. In economically quiet times, stability and pre-dictability are more highly valued than they are in periods of decline and unrest. During uncertain times, the ability to handle changing conditions becomes much more important. When more of the same doesn't work any more, there's a greater receptivity to trying something new. There are more challenges to the old order. Major corporations undergo seismic structural and management shifts. Creativity drives. Ideas take precedence over cre-dentials. That turbulence provides an opportunity to peo-ple who have previously been rejected or overlooked. The potential for true entrepreneurship is never greater than when the banks are the most frightened to lend the money to accommodate it.

Studies show there's no link between intelligence and creativity. We can all become more creative if we put our minds to it.

It's like the fellow who rolls into a Miami bank and says, "My wife suddenly decided to make a quick trip to the Bahamas and I need a fast three thousand dollars for one week."

The banker says, "But I don't know who you are. We have no history on you."

"Well," the fellow answers, "I'm a very successful real estate tycoon from New York City."

"That may be true, but I'd have to have some collat-eral."

"I have a brand new Cadillac sitting right outside."

"That's different," the banker says. He gladly gives

him the three thousand dollars and takes the Caddy for collateral.

Seven days later the New York businessman strolls in and pays the banker back his three thousand-dollar loan plus twenty-five dollars interest.

"Mister," says the banker, "I don't understand. I checked on you and found out you are a very successful real estate man. Why did you have to come in and borrow a paltry three thousand dollars?"

"Can you think of a better place to keep my car for seven days for only twenty-five dollars?"

The worst times can be the best times to launch your dream.

Bill Adams came back from Vietnam and went to work as a librarian in the Pittsburgh public schools, all the while scheming and dreaming of someday owning his own business. With ten thousand dollars inherited from his grandfather, he launched a business based on insulating windows by sticking on plastic bubble wrap attached by suction cups ... and wound up with a garage stacked with cartons of unsold materials. That naturally led to his next move, to find a way to get rid of the stuff. He noticed that small merchants tended to paste up notices on their windows with duct tape. Adams persuaded a gas station owner that the appearance of his place would improve if he substituted the suction cups. The station owner agreed, bought a few, and the rest is history. Adams is now the world's largest suction cup manufacturer, and while most businesses were hurt by the Persian Gulf War, Adams registered record sales, as slogans were being suction-cupped to windows across America.

Jeremy Kidson, twenty-eight, started his retail business with seven hundred dollars and a high school education. The *Naples* (Florida) *Daily News* reports that the sum total of his business training consisted of working at an auto repair shop in Berkeley, California. But he founded New West Design and now owns four of these clothing stores in San Francisco and Berkeley. In 1991, one of the roughest years in retail history, his sales grew 20 percent, to between four million and five million dollars.

His idea? "Upscale off-price," which, translated from retailer jargon, means that he sells fancy label designer clothes at discount prices, the perfect match between yuppie aspirations of grandeur and the recessionary reality of their new preoccupation with value. Kidson's greatest advantage was that he had not worked in a retail store until he owned one. He was never contaminated by conventional wisdom.

James Cannavino, now the head of IBM's Personal Systems Division, became a legend for the way in which he snared his first job at straitlaced Big Blue. According to the *New York Times,* Cannavino, a grocery clerk in Chicago in 1964, figured his best chance for landing a better job lay in the suburbs, so he rode a bus to the end of the line and walked into the first office he happened to see, which turned out to be IBM. Telling the receptionist he was there for a nonexistent interview, Cannavino bluffed his way into the manager's office, where, despite the lack of the required college degree, he talked his way into a job repairing keypunch machines by promising to work for nothing the first six months until he had proved he was the best keypunch repairman in the outfit.

Naturally, the systems-bound IBM had no system for accommodating such a unique proposition, so Cannavino was duly issued his paychecks, which he stashed uncashed. He lived off his side job as a pizza cook during the trial period at IBM. When the accounting department couldn't close its books because of his uncashed checks, Cannavino was given a permanent job, the foot on the ladder that was all he needed to start his climb to the top.

4. If you're an American, you live in the nation with the strongest, most dynamic economy in the world. Yes, yes, the Japanese and the Germans make and sell lots of wonderful cars and VCRs, and economists can throw statistics back and forth all day, but the true test of any free market is who wants in and who wants out. It's not human nature for people to scramble to get aboard a sinking ship. People still cast their most deeply felt votes with their feet, and despite our feeble attempts to limit immigration, those feet continue to take people to the United States.

American popular culture is the world standard for consumer preferences and conduct. Throughout the world, people dress the way they dress, behave the way they behave, think the way they think, because they are steeped in images of American soda pop, whiskey, blue jeans, and movies. English is the world language. The dollar is the world currency. Madonna and Arnold Schwarzenegger, a transplanted Austrian, are the worldwide choices as sex symbols.

Since 1970, we have created some forty million new jobs, our workforce has grown at a faster pace, both in absolute and percentage terms, than the workforces of both Germany and Japan. *Commentary* points out that "the U.S. holds more than 60 percent of the world market in computers, software, key peripherals (such as hard-disk drives and printers) and leading-edge microchips.... The U.S. has three times the computer power per capita of Japan or Europe.... In 1991, U.S. output of electronic systems was some $216 billion, almost twice Japan's production and nearly equal to Japan and Europe combined. The overall economic growth rate of 2.6 percent per year over the past two decades is above our 2 percent long-term historical average."

As for the much-reported decline in the quality of our

public services, it is hardly an unsolvable problem. We lack only the will to pay for it. Former French Foreign Minister Jean Francois-Poncer has said of our shabby public services, "They are not anything that could not be fixed by a 50 cent per gallon gasoline tax." If such a tax were adopted, over the screams and curses of American motorists, it would raise the price of gas here to roughly half of what it costs in Europe and Japan.

Which reminds me, food and housing here are also great bargains by world standards. Are you worried about having to give up the house for more economical, but cramped living quarters? Newly built Japanese houses average a thousand square feet, half the size of an average American home.

And then there's Russia. Last spring the government announced plans to more than double the minimum wage to 750 rubles per month (that's eight dollars). The government figures show that, with the raise, a person earning the new minimum wage now has about half the income necessary to buy the barest essentials of life.

5. Age is not the disadvantage it once was to employment. The era of the *linear* career ... school, work, retire at sixty-five, die at sixty-eight ... is over. As corporations rush to shed their high-salaried employees, you're probably going to be out of work much sooner than sixty-five. Yet, paradoxically, past sixty-five you're also much more likely to find work in some form for as long as you want it.

Given the ever greater intensity with which corporations now hire and fire, merge and acquire, restructure and dissolve, go public and go private, the likelihood of lifetime employment with a single company is becoming a memory. That trend is shown in the sharp increase in successful careers consisting of a series of short-term engagements. No longer is there any onus attached to a resume with more entries than John Gotti's rap sheet.

With this trend comes another change in attitudes: a decline in the loyalty of the corporation toward its employees and in the loyalty of the employees toward the corporation. It's like the difference in commitment made by the parties to a marriage contract as compared to a one-night stand. If you're not going to be around tomorrow, well, who cares what happens to you the day after tomorrow? In the economic relationship between employer and employee, this attitude translates into declines in both the supply and demand for corporate pensions and medical plans.

In 1988, the most recent year for which figures are available, only 38 percent of new jobs offered pensions, down from 43 percent in 1979. My guess is that the figures for '92 will show an additional decline to the low 30 percent area. In 1979, 23 percent of new jobs provided health insurance; in '88, the figure was down to 15 percent, and I predict another sharp drop when the '92 figures are out.

As a result, age is much less a barrier to employment than it used to be. You don't worry about employees getting old if you don't have to assume the obligations of their age and infirmities. All you care about is their ability to perform, here and now.

As cold-hearted as it seems, and is in economic terms, this change is opening up a whole new area of relatively well paid full- and part-time jobs for older workers who would otherwise be unemployable. Age is no longer the drawback it once was to employment. Retirement is no longer an age, it is an option. You can exercise it at *any* age … fifty-five, sixty-five, or seventy-five.

Still, aging is not without its drawbacks. Benjamin Franklin was elderly when he served as our ambassador to France. He was approached by a woman who indicated she was interested in more than his diplomatic moves. "Alas," said Franklin, "I am afraid I have reached the age where I can no longer take 'yes' for an answer."

6. Earlier, I mentioned the effects of your parents' longevity on your obligations to provide for them. While they're going to live longer than their parents did, given another generation of medical progress to build upon, so are you likely to live longer than your parents. And just as sixty-five is no longer the magic number it once was for retirement, neither is sixty-eight or sixty-nine or seventy. Your retirement years may nearly be equal to your career years.

What it adds up to is that just as your life itself is being extended, so is every part of your professional life cycle: education, career, retirement, obligations to parents and kids, periods of time free from obligations to parents and kids. All of it.

It means you have more time to prepare yourself financially and emotionally for retirement, but it also means that you have to be more careful in your planning, to be sure you don't outlive your money.

7. The law is on the side of people who are treated unfairly by their employers. Jury verdicts in wrongful discharge cases now average over $500,000 ... which is a hell of a lot more than twenty-six weeks of unemployment at $110 per. Good companies want neither the public embarrassment nor the financial damage of that kind of wallop.

In any situation where funny stuff is going on or your career is on the line, the best way to protect your interests is to create a contemporaneous written record of the events. If Anita Hill had done that instead of just telling a couple of her friends, Clarence Thomas might still be mowing his own lawn while remaining as a judge on the Court of Appeals and not on the Supreme Court.

Take your own notes. Make your own record. If you honestly feel you've been wrongfully discharged, if you are told you are being fired on the basis of your performance and you truly think your performance has been misjudged, if you've been discriminated against ... I suggest you may want to seek legal help.

There is also a growing intolerance toward intolerance. Plaintiffs who win verdicts under federal discrimination legislation can be awarded not only compensatory damages (loss of earnings) but punitive damages. Unrelated to any loss, these are granted to plaintiffs to emphasize the strong public policy against discrimination by punishing the employer economically. Ouch!

Plus, there is very little tolerance in the law for employers who discriminate or who permit sexual harassment on the job. Later in this book, you'll read about Lori Peterson, a twenty-eight-year-old attorney who's helping to create a whole new set of plaintiffs' rights in this area. The law is continuing to evolve in the employee's favor. By the year 2000, 57 percent of all new workers entering the workforce will be nonwhites, and 50 percent will be women. So those of us who are employers better get our act together before it's too late.

8. Changing values and expectations can erase the pain. In other societies, professions like the clergy, teaching, and social work are valued far more highly than in America. Yet, for a lot of us living in the most materialistic society on earth, success in material terms hasn't produced personal satisfaction. Who says you have to live by any values other than your own? If the personal freedom America affords has taught us anything, it's that you have only yourself to answer to for doing what you believe in and picking the life you choose.

After all, what have you lost? If it's a job, and you can't find one in your field, what about changing fields? Demanding, frightening, time-consuming, frustrating, but not terminal. Or moving to a more dynamic location? Costly, emotionally upsetting, and all of the above, but again, *not* terminal. Yet some people hang on and on with the same buggy-whip skills in the same permanently depressed areas.

Why try to preserve a "way of life" for yourself that no longer makes economic sense? Sooner or later the public patience with subsidizing your lifestyle is going to be exhausted. At one time, your job in steelmaking, in farming, in auto manufacturing may have been the backbone of America you thought it was. Thanks. It makes for great nostalgia, but what have you done lately? Americans are notoriously bad on history and short on gratitude.

If your system needs rewiring, the sooner you do it, the better off you'll be in the long run.

9. Corporate cast-offs are joining the ranks of entrepreneurs in increasing numbers. According to the *Miami Herald,* there are two principal reasons: first, by necessity, because the kind of corporate job they want just isn't out there, and second, because they've had their toes stepped on once too often in the corporate dance. This attitude runs from Executive Row down to the factory floor. It includes name-brand executives like Barry Diller, who left filmmaker 20th-Century-Fox to start his own entertainment company, and Peter Lynch, who quit as head of Fidelity's Magellan Fund at the top of the game to do freelance investment management and consulting, mostly on a volunteer basis, and more recently, Lynch's successor, Morris Smith, who, after two years, decided to do much the same thing in Israel. He is all of thirty-four years old.

It also includes less well known people like Don Lohr, forty-eight, who, after twenty-four years with Eastern Airlines, wound up on the street, hat in hand, when the company went out of business. He used his experience as a merchandising and sales manager to shift into an entrepreneurial role and start Local Motion Flea Market, Inc., a used auto and boat sales company. What made him do it? "Henry Ford said, 'Think you can. Think you can't.

Either way, you're right.' From Walt Disney, 'If you can dream it, you can do it.' I believe in all those silly positive sayings," said Lohr.

Not so silly when you can make them come true the way Lohr has.

10. Titles don't carry the weight they used to for white-collar workers.

Employees are becoming increasingly wise to the gambit of meaningless vice-presidencies in lieu of meaningful raises. Employers are tired of automatic annual wage increases for employees who perform as if their titles granted them hereditary rights.

The trend is *away* from the traditional reward, a higher rung on the corporate ladder, given in recognition of survival skills like seniority. This always meant snaring an increase in the departmental budget and adding new ranks of subordinates, the traditional measures of management ability.

The trend is *toward* paying for acquiring performance skills and achieving measurable goals.

Factory workers have long been paid on the basis of production and now, increasingly, are being given incentive pay to acquire additional skills. For instance, the *New York Times* reports that at Quaker Oats, new plant hires get their $8.75 hourly base pay increased to a top rate of $14.50 on the basis of learning new skills like driving a fork lift, rather than strictly on seniority.

Among white-collar people, salespeople always have been valued on this basis. They're paid when they sell and not paid when they don't. Who's going to lay off a salesperson who can demonstrate the ability to bring business in the door? Managers have a more difficult time of it in the new climate of white-collar shakeups and layoffs. How do you put a value on a good hire? Or a stirring letter to shareholders? Cutting-edge methods are now available to measure performance in even the more subjective areas, and researchers will keep refining their tools until they are able to gauge performance objectively rather than on the basis of office politics as usual. The more we get of that, the less we'll see of job titles as a basis of pay level.

11. Small business is providing the greatest number of new jobs. According to the Small Business Administration, from 1988 to 1990, larger businesses, those with five hundred or more employees, actually lost some 501,000 workers. During the same period, small business added 3,170,000 new jobs. This trend has continued through the recession. And the picture looks better than it ever has for women. 28 percent of all businesses in the U.S. are now owned by women, and by the end of 1992 women-owned businesses will employ more people than the entire Fortune 500!

12. Starting a small business isn't as labor- or capital-intensive as it used to be. Fax machines, personal computers, answering devices, printers, copiers, all the paraphernalia of the modern office means you can do everything you used to hire a secretary to do. Even make your own coffee.

6

HOW I GOT THE JOB I WANTED, #1

Recently, I ran an ad in a number of newspapers across the country asking people to describe in a letter how they got the job they wanted. From the hundreds of responses I received, I've selected some of the most original and creative. Here's the first.

While I was in college, an opening developed for an announcer on the local radio station to broadcast hockey games.

I wanted a job to earn some spending money, and I also was interested in getting experience in broadcasting. The only problem was that I had never seen a hockey game.

I tried to acquaint myself with the game a bit by

reading a short description of hockey in an encyclopedia, but I figured I would never learn enough about the sport to convince management to hire me, so I decided on another gambit.

Before arriving for the interview, I went to a local sporting goods store and rented a hockey helmet, pads, and other equipment, skates, and even a stick. I then dressed up as a hockey player, from head to toe, and tottered into the interview.

Seated across from the program director of the station, I looked like I had just walked in from the local hockey rink or from a Halloween party. The program director was stunned, and after a few perfunctory questions that I managed to fend off like a goalie blocking a net, I was given the job.

I started working three days later and, despite calling the puck a "ball" a few times, and occasionally referring to the rink as the "field," I managed to get through the game without too much difficulty. In fact, I continued broadcasting the team's games for the rest of the season, including a couple of road trips, and even through the first round of the playoffs before the team was eliminated.

I was invited back to do the games the following year, but I decided that I really didn't enjoy hockey that much. I figured that now that I was able to consistently refer to the "puck," "rink," and other elements of the game correctly, it was time to move on.

I spent the next year with my own DJ show, which propelled me into a short but enjoyable career in broadcasting. The experience taught me that enthusiasm and creativity can go a long way, often more so than experience and competency, in helping to land a job.

I am a forty-four-year-old man, currently an attorney, but formerly involved in journalism, including newspaper and magazine writing and broadcasting.

Marshall H. Tanick
Golden Valley, Minnesota

7

IF AT FIRST YOU DON'T SUCCEED ... YOU'RE DOING ABOUT AVERAGE: FIVE TIPS FOR BEATING REJECTION

1. *Ten setbacks are the going price for any worthwhile win.* If you look at the major league baseball standings at the end of any season, you'll find that, out of twenty-six teams, only four win their division, and only one of those four winds up winning the World Series. Every year, just four semiwinners and one top-of-the-heap winner out of twenty-six. Are those annual standings the end of the world for the twenty-two losers? Hardly. Because every season, there's another game of musical chairs, and you have a new set of winners and losers.

Sure, you may be down now, but that doesn't mean

the condition is permanent. American history is filled with legendary failures who pulled themselves up by the bootstraps and climbed to the top. Lincoln was a repeated business and political failure, losing bids for the state legislature, Congress (twice) and the Senate (twice), before he was elected president. Prior to the Civil War, Grant was a washout both as a clerk in his father's grocery store and as a lumber dealer. Harry Truman went bankrupt in the haberdashery business. What these gentlemen had in common was persistence and self-confidence. The harder they fell, the more determined it made them to get up off the deck and succeed.

2. *Analyze every failure, but never wallow in one*. Truman once said, "As soon as I realize I've made one damned fool mistake, I rush out and make another one." Failure is a condition all of us experience. It's our *reaction* to our failures that distinguishes winners from losers.

Like the fellow who remarked, "Of course I wasn't upset about being fired! I slept like a baby ... I cried all night."

What makes a great racehorse as compared to a cheap claimer is not just speed, it's heart. A claimer usually makes just one run. Once the horse is passed, that's it, the animal quits and the race is over. But stakes horses, the best of the breed, are different. Even if they're headed, they'll come back and try to regain the lead. There's no quit in them. Like Vince Lombardi's teams, they never lose, they just run out of time. Defeats are temporary. Heart and class are permanent.

3. *Don't rationalize away the hurt*. You didn't get the job? Turned down for a raise? Denied admission to the college of your choice? Don't kid yourself and try to cover up the hurt with "Gee, I didn't really want it anyway." Of course you wanted it. "I suppose I didn't deserve it." Of course you did. Self-delusion and self-hatred aren't the

answer. Don't let your worth be defined by others. Point your head in the right direction and get back in the game. Don't capitalize the hurt; expend it.

It's not a permanent condition, it's a short-term setback. You have a goal. The particular job or raise or school may have been a stepping stone to that goal, but that's all it was. There's more than one way to cross a river. Now you're going to have to rethink the path, but that doesn't mean you have to abandon the goal.

4. *Don't walk around as if you're wearing a scarlet letter.* For heaven's sake, who knows you were turned down for a job or for admission to Dartmouth? It's not going to be the lead story on the evening news. Rejection is only as big as you make it. Take an inventory of human emotional responses, like love, hate, greed, fear, jealousy, grief, envy, gratitude, compassion. Now compare them to self-pity. Of all the emotions on the list, some constructive, some not so constructive, I'd venture that self-pity probably has fewer positive applications, and can do less for you, than just about any of them. (Even jealousy? At least there's a pretty good torch song called "Jealousy." Can you imagine one called "Self-Pity"?)

Whatever you do, don't take rejection personally. It may have nothing at all to do with you.

A board member from a charitable organization went to call on a very wealthy man who hadn't given the organization a contribution in five years. As the visitor was talking to him about his social responsibilities and obligations, the millionaire interrupted, "Wait a minute! Do your records show my father is ninety years old and at his doctor's office once a week? My son has been out of work for two years. I have a widowed sister with five kids struggling to make ends meet. Now … if I don't help them, why should I help you?"

5. *Start worrying when they stop considering you as a contender.* Cary Grant, Marilyn Monroe, Alfred Hitchcock, Richard Burton, and Steven Spielberg—none ever won an Oscar. Babe Ruth was never named Most Valuable Player. Thomas Jefferson, John Quincy Adams, and Andrew Jackson all lost elections for the presidency before they won one. Losers?

No.

Legends.

II

READY?

8

GETTING A JOB *IS* A JOB. THE TEN THINGS YOU *MUST* DO TO FIND WORK

1. *Get a routine and stick to it.* Getting a job is not a nine-to-five job. It's a sixteen-hour-a-day proposition, from the moment you get up until the moment you go to sleep. With that kind of workload, you need a daily schedule to establish that routine and organize your time. This doesn't mean you're being sentenced to endless rounds of self-punishment and drudgery. If you're going to be at your best, you've got to have some fun, too, so make room for a little downtime.

Start the week unofficially on Sunday night. You'll want to scribble out a short list of things to get done the next week and check it against the list you had the previous week.

Set goals. To put them to work for you they must be:

Measurable
Identifiable
Attainable
Specific
In writing

And they need to be examined regularly.

How many new contacts did I make last week? Did I stretch out geographically into new areas? Explore new job descriptions? Improve my presentation or appearance? Grade yourself, and don't be too narrowly focused. A week without a job is not a week of failure. You may have accomplished other goals last week, things you've never had the time for or put in the effort to achieve in the past.

2. *Get back in shape.* Companies have always hired according to subtle, hidden values. Before the civil rights revolution, those values were not so subtle and hidden. Nonmale, non-WASPs who didn't give the right social signals need not apply. We like to believe that discrimination in the marketplace has been largely eliminated. Not so. Even though we have legislation that forbids hiring on the basis of race, religion, age, and gender, there are still millions of Americans who have no legal protection against job discrimination. Prejudice against overweight people seems to be the only form of discrimination that hasn't been made illegal, and it's practiced with a vengeance. All things being equal, studies have shown that the overweight have a much poorer chance of getting a job than people who are not overweight.

Under any circumstances, take huge pains with your makeup, hairstyling, and wardrobe. And not just at interviews, either. Looking good is the rule every time you poke your nose outside the door. If you're serious about getting a job, you're going to be visible in a number of ways where your appearance will be noted and can work for you or against you.

We're not all perfect tens, but there's a lot we can do to catapult ourselves up the scale. Appearance has always been 30 percent nature and 70 percent cunning artifice, so we can all be at least sevens if we try.

3. *Read.* Start with the local paper and the *Wall Street Journal.* The local paper gives you the classifieds, which are the meat and potatoes of your job search, and the *Wall Street Journal* is your link to the state of the national economy and the job market. Your job interviewer reads the *WSJ,* which is the best reason I can think of why you should, too. It also would be prudent to check out the business section of *USA Today,* as it often leads in identifying newtrends.

Here's a flash quiz that should give you a clue as to your priorities: What section of the paper do you read first? The sports page? *Doonesbury?* Your horoscope? When do you get around to the business news, looking specifically for developments in your field? Third? Fourth? Never? Your answer should tell you something about whether you've got your act together or not. Line up a few friends or relatives in other parts of the country to send you the classified sections from their Sunday papers. (Even though you can often get Sunday papers from cities all over the country at your airport or library, they seldom include the most precious section, the help wanted ads). Why would anyone in Tennessee want to see the classifieds in Clearwater? Well, maybe things are no go for nurses in Nashville but fabulous in Florida. Three or four Sunday classified sections from various parts of the country can give you a good feel for regional employment demand in your field.

It's not uncommon for an interviewer to ask the

"friendly" and "casual" question: "What have you been reading lately?" Have a good answer. Current business books and periodicals, trade and technical journals in your field, thoughtful books of any kind, fiction or nonfiction qualify, if you can discuss them creatively and analytically.

One job seeker took his efforts so seriously that he staggered home night after night bearing loads of books and periodicals to bone up for the next day's interviews. His little daughter couldn't understand and one day asked, "Mommy, why does Daddy always bring home all that work?" Her mother explained to the tot, "Well, darling, you see, Daddy has so much work to do and if he can't finish it during the day he brings it home." "Well," responded the daughter, "why don't they put him in a slower group?"

To stay current on your reading, you'll need to go to a bookstore for the most complete selection. As you might imagine, career books have become an area of explosive growth, so a little browsing should yield a wide range of choices and enable you to find several that meet your needs. There's a lot of specific advice out there on subjects like how to write a resume and how to handle an interview that can make the difference between a job and no job. Fond as I am of the library, don't rely on a dog-eared twenty-year-old book to fill in the gaps in your knowledge. There are current trends in hiring as in any other field, and you need to know what they are if you're going to be ahead of the pack.

The chief of police in a small city in Illinois recently applied for the chief's job in a bigger city. He was asked to fill out a questionnaire. Here's the first question, and his answer (in part), exactly as he wrote it.

Q: Discuss your management, budgeting, and administrative experience which you believe quali-

**fied you to serve as chief of a police department of
our size.**

A: ... As a police manager who holds an MBA degree,
I strongly believe that a progressive police agency may
also successfully use some of the corporate strategy of private business. For too long in police work, the "company"
has dictated what service the citizenry will have and how
they will receive it. In successful private enterprise, the
customer has a large say in what and how services will be
provided. This is why I read *Business Week* just as avidly
as *Police Chief.* Many practices of private enterprise can be
adapted by government agencies. Using corporate strategy, the police executive not only asks the community
what services it wants, but also what its priorities are.

Here's a guy who not only knows what to read, he
knows how to apply what he reads creatively to make a
point both about how police work should be performed
and about his own obvious professionalism.

Later on in the questionnaire they asked him what he
would do to keep morale high among the troops while
maintaining the appropriate level of discipline.

A: ... The policies of private sector companies articu-
lated in the book *In Search of Excellence* work splendidly
in the public sector as well. I attribute much of my success
in maintaining morale, while also increasing productivity,
to involving all employees in policymaking and decisions.

Hey, is this the kind of guy who's going to have trouble finding the job he wants? Of course not. In the traditionally unimaginative, structured, heavy-handed world of
police management, he's obviously ahead of the curve.
Anyone who can bridge the gap between *In Search of
Excellence* and in-search-of-dope-peddlers is a sure bet for
a big future.

Thirty years ago, female, minority, and college-graduate cops were unheard of. Today, they're not only commonplace, they're in leadership positions on police forces across the country. They speak the language of modern corporate America, like Willie Williams, the chief of the Los Angeles Police Department, who refers to the public as his "customers." You don't learn that by watching the cop shows on TV. You have to study and read.

4. *Make those calls.* Keeping your network alive means casting a wide net. Dive into your files and give yourself a quota of, say, five contacts a day. Be brief. Your agenda is obvious: What do you know that I don't that might provide me some work? It never hurts if you can carry your own weight and provide the persons you're calling with some information that may be of value to them. You might mention a hot sale they may not know about or some even hotter business gossip you may have picked up during your job hunt, like a major executive shuffle.

5. *Do your homework.* Stay on top of new developments in your field. For example, you may have been an art director at the same ad agency for the past fifteen years without having to learn how to use a computer for designing ads, but you're never going to get another job in advertising until you do. Now is the time to take those courses you never had time for ... and be sure you find a way to mention it during your interviews.

6. *Know the company you keep.* Before you interview, check with anyone you know who knows about the company: employees, customers, bankers, vendors. If you read my first book, *Swim with the Sharks Without Being Eaten Alive,* you know my passion for the library. Go to the business desk. The librarians there will locate newspaper clippings, magazine articles, advertising files, trade journals, and annual reports that describe the company. You're looking for two things:

Number one: You want clues to the company's reputation. Is it a leader in its industry? An also-ran? How does it compete? Does the company emphasize price? Quality? Service? Innovation?

Do you have any special strengths in any of these areas that you can bring to the table? If you do, don't forget to mention them during your interview.

A little while ago, the *Wall Street Journal* ran a guest column written by James Near, the president of Wendy's. He confessed that during the eighties, Wendy's had lost its way, becoming bottom-line oriented at the expense of the strengths that had built the company originally: concern for quality, service, and cleanliness for their customers; and training, benefits, and motivation for their employees. Once they got back to the basics, what Near called a "Mop Bucket Attitude," their earnings rebounded and the employee turnover was nearly halved. Now, it's no secret that many people don't regard employment in the fast food industry as a "real" job, but I'd be willing to bet that since the article appeared, Near has changed some minds about his company among job seekers and investors. Businesses that keep their focus on people have a way of being successful, whether they're dealing with employees or customers.

Number two: You want clues to the company's values and style. Be aware of the huge trend toward niche marketing, which is the concept of dividing the marketplace into even smaller segments in order to concentrate on a clearly defined target audience. A magazine like *Successful Meetings* is an example of a product designed around a niche market. The magazine serves as a vehicle for pinpointing marketing artillery at a small but identifiable and highly motivated market: the people who make their living as meeting planners, and the people who run hotels, airlines, travel agencies, convention facilities, speakers' bureaus, and catering services who act as vendors to meeting planners, and who have a need to advertise in a publication that reaches meeting planners.

Because of niche marketing, there are a lot of companies with highly idiosyncratic corporate styles, developed as a result of their adapting to the styles of the niche markets in which they sell their products or services. You wouldn't expect to find an atmosphere congenial to the Hell's Angels crowd among the employees at *Successful Meetings,* but you probably will find one, or its equivalent, at *Outlaw Bikers' Tattoo Revue.* (I swear on my sacred Kirby Puckett autographed official Little League baseball, there is such a magazine!) At *Successful Meetings,* tattooed outlaw biker types probably need not apply, and vice versa. The point being, you're going to find the best chance of getting a job ... and of being a success ... in a company where you fit in, tattoo-wise and otherwise.

Chuck Berry never solicited the New York Philharmonic for the chair of the first violinist. Know your field, consider the company you wish to keep, analyze your potential employer, and examine the audience. There are other things to consider. Some companies are wild about teamwork. These companies tend to hire type-B personalities with strong people skills, a willingness to submerge personal goals to team goals, and with the patience to handle corporate bureaucracy. Other companies want Type-As, assertive people, hard-chargers who are willing to ruffle a few feathers if it means getting the job done better.

Corporate attitudes toward politics have changed. Companies that used to fear being publicly identified with any cause more controversial than the Girl Scout cookie campaigns are becoming outspoken on a variety of heavy-duty social concerns, from race to abortion to AIDS. The sixties generation never saw much point in separating their personal and political lives. The issues that animated these people as college activists are finding their way onto the agendas of the corporations they now manage. If they offend a certain number of potential customers, well, so be it.

The executives at these companies are willing to risk paying that price in exchange for the satisfaction they get from using their corporate power to flex their political muscle and the commitment and fierce loyalty they gain from customers who share their views.

Because of the growing segmentation of the marketplace, several of the companies that have taken the boldest stands have been able to eat their cake and have it, too, a la mode. Ben and Jerry's Ice Cream is committed to a wide range of liberal social issues. Benetton, the clothing chain, has run a series of ads featuring international and interracial groups. The Body Shop (cosmetics) favors environmental causes.

While the more outspoken companies are largely on the left, many companies still work the conservative side of the street. Instead of incorporating their views in their advertising or in their image building, the right-wing oriented companies tend to make their mark by contributing, through their PACs, to conservative candidates and causes. The Mobil Corporation has been an exception. Mobil has generated a lot of attention with a series of newspaper ads designed as editorial-style essays generally supportive of conservative positions.

Whichever way these companies swing, if they're politically hot, you'll want to know it before you interview. Whether you yourself are politically hot or politically not, your best bet is a job where the corporate style meshes with your own.

Corporate style is not just a matter of politics. If you're a guy with a beard, better get a closer shave before you fill out an application at Domino's. This firm considers beards unsuitable for people working in the food preparation business.

Then there is the classic example of all time, which I've told before. Years ago, no male employee at IBM dared to wear anything but a white shirt. One day, the boss, the legendary Thomas Watson, came to work in a blue shirt.

"What do you think?" said one of the underlings to another.

"Better not try it," said his buddy, "It could be a trick."

7. *Thank you. Thank you. Thank you.* Did you have a little chat with the receptionist or with a secretary while you were waiting for one of your interviews today? Write down that name and send a thank-you note recalling the conversation. It'll help differentiate you from the pack when you call that firm, and it won't hurt your chances of having those calls put through, either. And, of course, the interviewer and anyone else you may have met at the company are musts on your list, as are any of the contacts you made during the day. For the past thirty years I have strongly recommended you hand-carry your thank-you notes back to the interviewers the same day.

You may think this is tedious and unnecessary busy-work. It isn't. George Bush wrote an endless stream of short notes over the decades as he made his way, step by step, up the political ladder. *Time* magazine called it "Rolodex Diplomacy." If it could help him get elected president of the United States, it can help you get a job.

8. *Keep notes.* The Mackay 22 (chapter 33) is only one ingredient. You're going to want to have a record of *all* your day's meetings and calls, so when you follow up later, you know what was said, what personal information

might be useful in your next conversation, and what your strategy is for your next contact. If you think I'm a nut about keeping records, let me remind you that this is the first generation that really has gotten out of that habit. Until recently, everyone wrote everything down. When Napoleon wanted to tell Josephine how much he cared, he didn't say it with flowers or send a candygram, he wrote a letter (and used an envelope).

Mozart wrote a few thousand letters, many of which survive today. When Wolfgang Amadeus wanted an advance from his publisher, he couldn't pick up the phone and call. He had to write. You need accurate records of who said what to whom.

No matter who you are, no matter what you do, you need a system for keeping track of people. When I started in business, I kept a well-worn business card file that I thumbed through on a daily basis. When the backs of the cards were so covered with smudges and chicken scratch-ings that they became unreadable, I developed a system on paper where I could make regular notations to my cus-tomer files. That evolved into the Mackay 66, which you may be using now or have already read about.

Whether it's a daily diary, an old address book, a Rolodex, or one of the new contact management com-puter programs, you need something to keep you orga-nized. Start now and keep track of everyone you meet, making note of when and how you met them and what you learned about them. If you are unemployed, you'll be doing part of this from memory, putting together a log of everybody you've ever known who you think can help you. If you are employed now, you have a great opportu-nity to start your contact file. So get started. And never quit.

9. *Volunteer.* Get involved in a cause that means something to you, whether it's politics, the Symphony

Fund Drive, United Way, Alumni Fund Drive, Save the Whales, what have you. First, you're keeping actively busy during an emotional downturn in your life. Good for the head.

Second, you're improving your job-hunting skills. Volunteering involves marketing, selling, time management, public speaking, fundraising, creativity. What could be more targeted to your needs than learning, practicing, polishing your strengths, and overcoming your weaknesses? I would *never* have learned to sell if I hadn't been a volunteer trying to raise money for countless causes.

It's the best sales training boot camp there is, it's free, and no one, that is, *no one,* wants to do it, because no one wants to hear ten trillion "no"s.

Are you uncomfortable speaking in public? Volunteering can provide you with the experience you need. Before I became involved as a volunteer in building support for a domed stadium in Minneapolis, I'd have been lucky to get asked to introduce the introducer at a PTA meeting. I ended up making close to one hundred speeches a year during the seven years we fought for that project. My speaking schedule is now so full, I've started making notes for books on the margins of my speeches.

Third, depending on the organization and the role you take, volunteering will put you in contact with some of the most important people in your community. They'll see you do your stuff. (Do I hear you flipping the pages of your Rolodex or pressing the keys of your personal computer already?)

Fourth, and not least in importance, you'll be doing your community a service you can be proud of. And if volunteering pays off in no other way than this, it's well worth the time and effort. It's good for the soul. Potential employers know that people who do volunteer work make loyal and dedicated employees, so get that volunteer service into your resume, and better yet, mention it in your interviews, too.

10. *Get ready for tomorrow.* Clothes in shape? Appointments confirmed? Schedule set? Sign off. You've had a busy day.

9

WHAT DO LEE IACOCCA, SALLY JESSY RAPHAEL, LUCIANO PAVAROTTI, BORIS YELTSIN, AND DR. OLIVER SACKS ALL HAVE IN COMMON WITH TEN MILLION OTHER AMERICANS?

They've been "dehired."

Or, from "A Litany of Euphemisms for 'You're Fired,'" which appeared in *Executive Recruiter News,* they have experienced:

Outplacement
Downsizing
Rightsizing

Force reduction
Work force adjustment
Indefinite idling
Redundancy elimination
Involuntary separation
Skill-mix adjustment
Work force imbalance correction
Chemistry change
Negotiated departure
Redeployment
Destaffing
Degrowing
Dismissal
Axed
Canned
Let go
Deselected
Decruited
Excessed
Transitioned
Vocational relocation
Release
Selective separation
Coerced transition
Executive culling
Personnel surplus reduction
Career assessment and reemployment
Fumigation

According to *Sports Illustrated,* eight out of ten Americans will be fired at least once. As anyone who has been fired can tell you, the experience ranks right down there with the death of a loved one or divorce, because it affects not only your income and your family's well-being but your own sense of personal worth.

No matter how well handled or how badly bungled, there is no way to escape entirely unscathed.

But remember that eight-out-of-ten figure. You've got some excellent company.

Lee Iacocca was booted out of the presidency of Ford Motor Company by its chairman, Henry Ford II, in July 1978. Ford, who will probably be remembered best for having coined the phrase "Never complain, never explain" when he was arrested for speeding while in the company of a lady not his wife, was totally in character regarding Iacocca's dismissal. "It's my name on the building," said Ford. Iacocca went on to win such acclaim for his revival of the dying Chrysler Corporation that in 1988 he was even touted as a possible presidential candidate.

Sally Jessy Raphael, by her own count, was handed the pink slip no fewer than eighteen times while building a career in talk radio. Determined to make a go of it no matter how long it took, she and her husband developed a regular routine each time she was dumped. They would pack up the car, tell the kids it was time to visit some more Civil War battlefields and go camping, and off they would trot to the next gig, living in the station wagon until a paycheck finally kicked in.

In 1989, Luciano Pavarotti was fired from the Lyric Opera of Chicago. He missed twenty-six out of forty-one scheduled appearances that season. Fame and talent don't protect anyone these days, not even the world's most popular operatic tenor, from getting the hook.

Boris Yeltsin was a mere Gorbachev protégé in 1987, an upstart with a mind and personality of his own, and just a bit too visible and critical for the boss's taste. After a really nasty session in which he was chewed out, up, down, and around for his lack of support of his mentor, Yeltsin was fired from his position as head of the Moscow Communist Party. But despite the public disgrace, Yeltsin rose from the ashes to hold off the attempted August 1991 coup against Gorbachev. His courage and steady nerves captured the public's imagination and he quickly displaced his former boss. Now Yeltsin is president of Russia and it's Gorby who is on the bench plotting his comeback.

Dr. Oliver Sacks is the author of *Awakenings* and *The Man Who Mistook His Wife for a Hat*. He's also a neurologist who was laid off in 1991 from his position at the Bronx Psychiatric Center, where he had worked for twenty-four years. Budget cutbacks did in this gifted and versatile doctor, as they did in more than a thousand other mental health workers who were let go at the same time. Being a best-selling author didn't save him. In fact, it might have made the decision easier for his superiors, making it possible for them to rationalize that he could always write books.

None of these talented people "deserved" to be fired. But they were. It's no sin. No disgrace. It can happen to anyone, and 80 percent of the time, it has.

This is something worth repeating. Remember your Nietzsche: "That which does not kill me makes me stronger."

10

CONFESSIONS OF A FLASHER

Our minds are working even when we think they're not. They function like very sophisticated computers. Or, more accurately, very sophisticated computers have reached the point where they function like very primitive minds. Give your mind a problem, and though you may not realize it, the machinery keeps chugging away, unnoticed, beneath the surface, until suddenly, a solution erupts into your consciousness.

And there you are, it's a) three o'clock in the morning, b) halfway into your commute to work, or c) in the middle of dinner with your rich Aunt Bea and her less than enthralling recitation of the high points of her trip to Toledo (not the one in Spain). You know you have to get the idea down on paper or into a dictating machine or you're going to lose it forever.

Because much of this book and the others were written from mindbursts like these, I've learned never to be without paper and pencil or a tape recorder.

In my opinion, it's a good habit for almost anyone who has to think for a living. My wife particularly appreciates it, since she no longer has to be sure to give me a paper napkin when we are having a dinner party at home, so I won't ruin the good linen.

Looking for a job is tough, grinding mental work. You have to make it your number-one priority if you're going to reach your goal. Put your powers of concentration into gear, get focused, and your mind, running on automatic pilot, will do a lot of the grunt work.

Many of the ideas you read here will not seem immediately relevant to your situation, and then, days, even months, after you've read them, your mind may make a connection between this material and something that's going on in your life. In a flash, a powerful idea will roll out of your head and drop into your lap. Leave yourself open to that possibility. Take the time to turn inward, to review your thoughts and experiences, to give your mind a chance to do its work.

I wish I'd said it first … a mind is a terrible thing to waste … especially on someone who refuses to use it. Or, as Robert Frost said, "The brain is a wonderful organ; it starts the moment you get up in the morning and does not stop until you get to the office."

11

HIT THE ROAD, JACK

If you've heard that before, it may have been your former boss bidding you a fond farewell from the company payroll. However, when some companies boot their employees out the door, they have a different purpose in mind.

Once a year, Hyatt Hotels shuts its corporate doors and dispatches 550 top executives to the company's 105 hotel properties around the world. They're not assigned to loll about in the presidential suites gauging the state of Hyatt's VIP service. They go where the rubber meets the road, making beds, washing dishes, and parking cars (at least they get to keep the tips). This top management team wants to get a hands-on feel, to touch the pulse of the marketplace. How can anyone manage a "hospitality" business unless he or she appreciates what kind of effort it takes the employees to deliver service to the consumer at the most fundamental level?

No hotel chain has ever been able to figure out how to motivate a beleaguered bellhop or an unwilling waitress into behaving like a bouncing, eager teenager, but at least Hyatt people understand why their employees' feet hurt.

And so it is with pounding the pavement for a job. If you're applying at Nike for a marketing job, or even an accounting position, go out into the real world and see what it takes to sell a pair of running shoes. Find a shoe dog who'll let you study at his feet while he flogs his Nikes, Reeboks, and L.A. Gears. If you're applying for a job as a sales manager at Carlson Travel Network, then talk to travel agents, those of the Carlson persuasion as well as their competitors. How can you expect to land a job as a manager of a business if you haven't studied the business at the marketplace level, where company and customer intersect, where the product rolls off the line?

This is the Hyatt approach, and it works, because no matter where you apply, you've leapfrogged into the finals. How many applicants take the trouble to do this? About 2 percent, tops.

Any guesses on which 2 percent get the jobs?

12

JOB HUNTING IS A CONTACT SPORT

When Britannia ruled the waves, the British used to send battleships steaming up and down the harbors of lesser powers as a way of ensuring that their opinions would be respected. It was called "showing the flag." Usually it spared the British the trouble of kicking sand in the little guy's face.

Making others aware of your presence is still an effective job-hunting and job-holding tactic, and you can use it without firing a single shot.

More and more jobs are being filled these days by headhunters, politely known as management recruiters. It pays to make yourself known to them. If these potential gatekeepers could be influential at some time in your career, shouldn't you be digging your well before you're thirsty and trying to lay some groundwork with them?

Here's how to make contact and to make the contact pay off:

1. Make your annual convention or trade show appearance more than a junket. Headhunters swarm over these like flies on a warm, wet Eskimo Pie. This time when you take the trip to Las Vegas, stay out of the casinos and pay attention to the name badges so you can learn who the specialists are in your field and introduce yourself.

2. Use the career change columns in your industry's trade journals. If someone has jumped ship from one company to another in order to fill an important position, chances are a competent pro may have had a hand in the move. Take the newly placed person to lunch. Do the "a friend of mine is considering a career change" number, and if they open up, find out if and who the headhunter was. Now you've got a reason to ...

3. Congratulate headhunters on their own career advances. Give them a call. Drop them a note. No one ever got angry at a well-earned compliment. They have egos, too. And they're likely to remember someone who took the trouble to reach out and touch them.

4. Be visible. Keeping a low profile is for guys ducking bullets. You want the world to be aware of your progress. Just completed an advanced management training course? Been promoted? Broadened your responsibility? Who's going to know if you don't tell them?

When you toot your horn, don't save it for a few lines in your annual Christmas letter right after the paragraph about Johnny's two new molars. Develop your own mailing list. Include headhunters. Send out the newspaper clipping or the news release. If there isn't one, write a short note announcing how pleased and happy you are with your new credentials. The information you mail out is going into files that could be as important to you as your credit report and always makes a lot better reading.

5. Be a resource. Now that you've got a headhunter's name on your Rolodex, make sure your name is on theirs. Make it known that you'll be happy to assist them in their searches, coming up with names of possible candidates or companies. By helping them for now, you've helped yourself for later.

6. Take a chance on romance. Even if you're secure in your job and not seeking to make a switch, you may change your mind if the right opportunity comes along. If a recruiter offers you a discreet interview with someone who has expressed an interest in you, consider exploring the jungle. You could be pleasantly surprised.

7. Never, ever treat a recruiter rudely. They have very long memories. The recruiter you dump on today could be the person you're calling tomorrow or next week for help in finding a job. Do you think that person will be eager to return your call after you've banged the phone down in his ear? There's always another candidate. Burn your bridges and you're going to be looking for a life raft.

13

THEY CAN'T HIRE YOU
IF THEY DON'T KNOW WHO YOU ARE

Okay, so you don't like headhunters. Since you realize that a lot of companies are filling key positions from outside, you still want to get noticed by other potential employers. Someday the red tag may show up in your locker. Someday you might have just the vital statistics another company needs. This one is for the do-it-yourselfer. Let's twist the tail of the last chapter a little and come up with a game plan.

1. This time when you go to trade conventions, you're going to be concentrating on meeting the top players among your principal competitors. Do your homework, *à la* the Mackay 66 in *Swim with the Sharks,* and learn

where their personal interests lie. Now you have a couple of minutes of dazzling smalltalk. When you can riff on their hometowns and the schools they attended, they'll be saying to themselves, "Who is that masked man?"

2. Get involved in industry associations. They're perfect cover for being in contact with just about anyone in your industry. Even if you're an adversary, bombing positions that your competitors hold near and dear, you'll be remembered for tenacity and dedication. More than once, I've gone into a bargaining session and lost big-time, yet I wound up with such admiration and respect for the lawyer on the other side, I hired that person the next time I was facing a tough negotiation.

3. Do your community work where it can do the community—and you—the most good. If you want to be visible to other companies, you have to go where the ducks are.

Companies are being bombarded by requests for volunteer help from all directions. Pick a cause that your company may not be deeply involved in but one that is being backed to the hilt by another company in your industry. Inside, you'll be seen as someone who's taken on a thankless task. You're taking the weight for a cause your own folks have written off. Outside, you're showing your face where you'll be seen by others in your industry.

4. Become the name on every Rolodex or personal computer in town. Trade journals are salivating for articles by industry writers. Business writers, reporters, securities analysts, and academic types are always in need of pithy remarks and reliable industry statistics. That's you. Establish yourself as an industry expert. The best way to prove that you're not is to stay safe and secure, hidden in your own little corner of your own little nest, your only public appearances coming on your way to and from the parking lot.

5. Don't accidentally go into hiding. If you're a married woman, make sure your name is listed in the phone book separately from your husband's, at least with your initial. Recruiters aren't happy about having to call you at the office to discuss your next career move. Even if you're the only person in the Western Hemisphere who can dip her finger into a pot of number 10 envelope glue and tell that it's done cooking, no one is going to plow through twenty-three pages of Andersons set in six-point type in the local phone directory to find out which one you're married to.

And male or female, if you move or are relocated, make sure that the important industry types in your old area know your new home address and phone number.

More people have been hired by being in the right place at the right time than for any other single reason. But you can't take advantage of that unless the person doing the hiring knows who and where you are. I'd love to hire "The Invisible Man" to sit in at my competitors' sales meetings, but no one can tell me how to find him.

14

IT ISN'T WHO YOU KNOW AND IT ISN'T WHAT YOU KNOW... IT'S WHAT YOU KNOW ABOUT WHO YOU KNOW

A startling statistic appeared recently in the *National Business Employment Weekly:* a survey of fifteen hundred successful job hunters shows that 63 percent found new positions through personal contacts of one kind or another; 11 percent through ads, and only 2 percent by sending in unsolicited resumes.

People who pooh-pooh the importance of "contacts" and "networking" as business tools tend to regard them as either the evil workings of an establishment conspiracy against superior but less well-connected talent or as the tacky device of an army of polyester-clad Babbitts, schmoozing their way through backslapping sessions while reaching into each other's pockets with their free hands.

A reality check reveals a different picture. My father made his living for forty-five years as a newspaperman. He couldn't have survived a day without contacts. For journalists, contacts are so vital they have their own jargon for them: "sources." It's been estimated that over 85 percent of all news stories are based on information provided by sources, whether calling in tips and ideas to reporters or serving as resources for quotes and expert opinion. In journalistic circles, a good reporter is often defined more by the strength of his or her Rolodex than by his or her writing skills.

On a less specialized level, contacts also can mean the difference between success and failure.

My daughter Jojo, who was majoring in dance at the University of Michigan, called one day to tell me that it was a matter of life and death that she land the hottest job on campus for the next semester.

What was this dream job?

Hostess at a beer joint.

Question: Why was standing around a noisy room for hours at a time at minimum wages, passing out menus offering nothing but burgers, double burgers, and double double super burgers, anyone's idea of the height of glamour?

Answer: Why can't parents ever get it?

Whatever its hidden charms, the place was the number-one campus hangout at the time, and to be seen there, let alone have the showcase position at the head of the receiving line, was to be anointed semiofficial chief social arbiter of the campus and surrounding metropolitan area.

How do you get picked when there are 137 other applicants who want the same job?

You apply the concept that is the number-one sales clincher of all time: You figure out what it is you can do for your customer or prospective employer that others can't do … or hadn't thought of.

"How many students are there in your dance classes?" I asked.

"Forty-five," she answered.

"How many women in your sorority?"

"Ninety-five."

"How many guys in your boyfriend's fraternity?"

"A hundred twenty."

"Will he help you get the job?"

"He better."

"All right, then, that's 260 solid contacts. Done deal," I said. "At the interview you proudly whip out the rosters of your sorority, your dance classes, and your boyfriend's fraternity. Paint a picture. If you are hired, your plan, strategy, and promise is to personally contact every name on that list and make sure they come and visit you on your new job and, obviously, eat and drink there. Then, for the knockout punch, unleash your Rolodex of three and a half years on campus and show the manager that you have five hundred names on it in addition to the Greeks, and then tell the manager you'll also work that list."

She got the job.

She delivered the bodies.

She won because she was prepared to win.

Was she the best menu-passer-outer, reservation-taker, and seating-chart-organizer that beer and burger emporium could have hired? Who knows?

No one ever said life was fair. What is true is that life does not pay off on fairness, it pays off on results. And because Jojo had learned that and was prepared to deliver the kind of results that her prospective employer wanted, she got what she wanted and he got what he wanted.

Preparation is also the key to taking the pressure off yourself and putting it on the other guy. The best way I ever heard it described was by Lee Trevino.

"I've been playing golf for money since I was old enough to see over the top of a tee, and I know what pressure is. Pressure isn't playing your third sudden death hole in the last round of the Master's.

"You only get that far if you're totally in control and unshakable. And you know it. You've prepared for anything, absolutely anything the gods of golf can throw at you. Pressure is when you've got thirty-five bucks riding on a four-foot putt and you've only got five dollars to your name."

Be prepared and you can handle anything.

15

HOW I GOT THE JOB I WANTED, #2

Richard Arlook, a great agent who is lucky enough to have my son, David, as a client, and vice versa, sent me this letter.

When I came to California in 1983 after graduating from college, I didn't know anyone in the film industry. As everyone knows, getting a job in the entertainment field is incredibly difficult unless you have a personal connection to someone in the business. Without a contact you need to find other, more innovative ways to get your foot in the door. Though I was fortunate to land an entry-level position in television right out of college, my real goal was to work in the film business.

But despite the fact that the Century City building I worked in was surrounded by major studios and some of Hollywood's top producers, distributors, and talent agencies, I really wasn't getting any closer to the people who could offer me a job. What's more, I knew I was one of maybe a million people who shared the same goal: getting a job in a business that's known for being closed to outsiders.

So here's what I did: I had been getting my hair cut in the barber shop in the lobby of the building where I worked and I noticed a lot of studio execs and producers getting their hair cut there as well. Since I had gotten friendly with the owner of the shop, I gave him a stack of my resumes and asked him to personally place them in the hands of these "big wigs" while he had their undivided attention. Fortunately, he liked me so much he not only gave them my resume, he also included an enthusiastic pitch about what a talented, industrious, and hardworking young man I was. (Kind of brings new meaning to the word headhunter.)

Anyway, I'm sure more than a few of these big shots smiled politely, brought my resume back to their office, and dropped it in the circular file. But none of that mattered, because about two weeks later the manicurist came running into my office saying, "There's a producer downstairs who wants to meet you." I hurried down to the lobby where I came face to face with a real live Hollywood producer who was looking to fill a position in his company. He set me up with a formal interview with his vice-president. I got the job, rose through the ranks of the company, and eventually used that position as a springboard for a job at a major studio.

Richard Arlook
Beverly Hills, California

(Mr. Arlook is an agent with The Gersh Agency in Beverly Hills. He represents writers, directors, and producers in the motion picture and television industry.)

III

AIM...

16

YOU CAN'T TELL A COVER BY THE BOOK

Did you ever take one of those blindfold tests in which you try to identify different brands of the same product? If you have, you've probably found that you can't tell your favorite brand from the others, even though you may have been a loyal consumer for years.

Brand name marketing is the enormously successful and sophisticated method of convincing you to buy one particular product that is essentially indistinguishable from another competing product. It's done through shrewdly constructed advertising, packaging, pricing, and distribution strategies. How does a small beer company compete with the big, national brands that are available everywhere and sold in every size, shape, and alcohol content, from seven-ounce "pony" bottles of 3.2 to kegs of strong beer? They specialize. They segment the market. Such and such a beer is for elite types who wouldn't dream of being seen drinking a beer made for the masses. Another bears a label that carries a well-known local connection and is only sold regionally. Another is found only by scrounging around on the bottom shelves at low-rent liquor stores.

Brand after brand after brand. And it doesn't matter that they are all brewed by the same company and come from the same barrel.

Now hold that thought for a moment. We'll be right back.

My wife, Carol Ann, who has taught art history, recently told me that from the time the first caveman "Rembrandt" scratched a picture on his living room wall until Pablo Picasso and cubism changed the world of art, artists and their perspective paintings insisted on a single point of view. Cubism changed that forever. Cubists painted their subjects from many positions on the same canvas, so that heads, noses, and eyes were seen simultaneously in profile and full face. In doing this the cubists showed us that there are many different realities and that all of them are equally true or real.

Well, that's semi-interesting. Modern marketing. Modern art. What does that have to do with jobs? Just this: There's more than one reality about how to package a job or even how to get one. Your success can depend as much upon your imagination and your creativity as it can upon your performance skills.

Take an entry-level position, for example. From the potential employer's perspective, what's there to make you stand out from a hundred other applicants? Unless you are somehow able to enhance the underlying product through marketing, packaging, pricing, or distribution and thereby give the employer's chair a spin, you're indistinguishable from the others.

Six months ago, a super young woman named Cathy Paper stumbled into my office, downhearted and discouraged. A 1989 Williams graduate, she was a top student and was finding it very difficult to navigate even in the slow lane, let alone in the fast lane.

Twelve months of looking and an 0-for-100 job-hunting success ratio with local ad agencies plopped her into an interview with me for advice.

We talked for a while and I was so impressed that I helped her get an interview at her dream agency, an agency that hadn't previously responded to her mailed-in resume.

Do you see what's happening here? When the "product," Cathy Paper, was "packaged" like every other product … a resume that came in over the transom one Monday morning with a hundred other resumes … she didn't get a nibble. So Cathy decided to get someone to redesign the package. That's me. I'm the "repackager." She used my advice to help her leapfrog the recognition hurdle and get noticed by her target market, the "consumer," a potential employer.

At her interview, Cathy offered to work six months for free. Now, we have a new element, an almost irresistible "pricing" strategy at work. Free offer. Try a sample. If you like the product, maybe you'll buy it.

Two interviews later at the same agency, they offered her a job. It wasn't quite the job she wanted, and her offer to work for nothing was refused. Instead, she was given a subentry-level job at a big six dollars an hour, but still, you can't get dealt a straight flush unless you're in the game. Three months later, I got an up-beat, excited call from Pat Fallon, the head of the agency. "Everybody loves Cathy Paper at work and she's a dynamo. Can't miss. What a find! She's going on the regular payroll immediately. Thanks for bringing her to our attention."

Repackaging and a clever pricing strategy let them see the Cathy Paper product in a new perspective. She made the sale. She got the job.

Lou Holtz, one of the most successful college football coaches in history, barely made the football team in high school. He weighed 106 pounds and wore Coke-bottle glasses. But Holtz was focused and he was determined to play football. He learned all eleven positions, just in case some starter got tired enough or beat-up enough, and then their substitute got tired enough or beat-up enough, so that he could get into the game. As a sixteen-year-old high school kid, he was, I'm sure, not big on marketing theory, but by being available in any size, shape, or configuration he was the "nationally advertised brand." Maybe not first-string quality, but he was there anywhere, anytime, anyplace they needed him.

Make yourself so valuable you know everybody's job. You could not only save your own job, you could even wind up like Holtz, coaching the whole team.

You're the product. If you're not selling, it's time to rethink your marketing strategy, to recast yourself in such a way that you're seen in a different perspective. Re-create reality. It will help you get the job you want and keep the job you love.

17

PREPARE TO MAKE A SPECTACLE
OF YOURSELF

According to some job advisers, if you don't look and act like the president of the local Young Republican Club at your job interview, you stand about as much chance of getting the job as you would if you'd shown up at the Coronation Ball *au naturel* and asked the queen for a dance. You'll be noticed, but for all the wrong reasons. Their idea seems to be that the more you blend into the woodwork, the better chance you have of landing the job.

I don't buy it.

One of our local papers, *Skyway News,* recently reported how offbeat tactics can pay off in jobs.

• Rose Hinchey had been out of work for four months when she saw an ad for her dream job with a local TV station. The standard tactic, a cover letter with a copy of her resume, netted absolutely nothing. So she launched a more imaginative campaign, which included letters from the fellow she was going with, from her lawyer, from her eighty-year-old mother, even from her priest, who wrote, "I'm enclosing this in hopes that you will hire Miss Hinchey. It's depressing to look at her sad face, and besides, we haven't had a donation from her in months." She was hired.

• A candidate for a teaching job with the Minneapolis public schools sent a singing telegram praising her skills. "When people sell themselves in a creative way," said Dan Loewenson, who hired her, "it does attract attention."

• Brian Spanier, another imaginative applicant, won a job at Chuck Ruhr Advertising after sending the company a creative mailer. On the cover was a teaser headline that read: "One out of 89 people in Spring Hill, Minnesota, aspires to be an art director." When the cover was opened, the inside page showed a photo of Spanier, standing next to a road sign that read "Spring Hill, population 89" with copy underneath reading, "I'm the one." His imagination won him his first job in advertising.

Two years ago, I attended a graduation ceremony at the University of Michigan at Chrysler Arena with eighteen thousand other people. Seated up in the rafters, I watched thousands of seniors parade across the stage collecting their sheepskins. Suddenly, a roar went up from the crowd. (Had Ohio State just conceded the Big Ten football title four months in advance of the season? Not yet.)

A female graduate had walked across the stage with a placard on the top of her graduation cap. In huge white letters on the placard were the words ... I NEED A JOB. As soon as the program ended, people were falling all over themselves to give her their business cards. Did she land a job because of her ingenuity? I don't know, but I do know that 8,333 graduates without jobs sure wished they had thought of it first.

Creativity in business always pays off, not just in acquiring jobs. In 1991 when I was asked to deliver the commencement speech at the Penn State MBA graduation, I tried to figure out what I could do to escape that assembly-line look that seems to make so many commencement speeches resemble a day's output at the Model T factory. Two weeks before I was scheduled to speak, I put on a wig and horn-rimmed glasses and, posing as my student-host's Uncle Willie, descended on the campus to do my research for the talk. I went to classes, conversed with students and faculty, stood in line, eating, reading, talking, listening ... like a Penn State student. And that was my line of attack, not "I have seen the future, I have seen the leaders of tomorrow, and I have seen you looking at your watches, so come up and get your diplomas," but more along the lines of "I have seen Penn State, and here's what I think the world looks like from your perspective." It seemed to work. My wife sat next to a professor who told her it was the first time he had ever seen MBA students taking notes at their own graduation.

Does creativity always work? Certainly not. Inventive self-promotion undoubtedly works best in applying for creative jobs. If you're looking to be hired as a sewer engineer, it's doubtful the person reviewing your application is in the market for people with funny remarks to make about sewer work. And, be forewarned: Creative means original, not copycat, ideas. Be ingenious, not imitative.

Take the case of finding a marketing director for the

new civic arena here in Minneapolis called Target Center, where professional basketball is played. Karyn Gruenberg says when she advertised for the position, three different applicants responded by sending her a sneaker with a comment that read, "Now that I've got one foot in the door, how about the other?"

Creativity does not come in threes; you'd better be flying solo.

I think the best strategy you can follow is to try to separate yourself from the pack.

There's a man named Barnett Lipton who's made a nice career out of this concept. He calls it the *WOW* factor. Lipton produces spectacles. Not the kind you look through, but the kind you look at. He produced the opening ceremonies for the 1984 Olympics and the 1990 U.S. Olympic Festival and has done the half-time shows for several Super Bowls.

When I asked him about his strategy for winning over an audience, he said, "I want five *WOW*s. Five untoppable, unstoppable, unforgettable special effects." Lipton knows that the only way to create that kind of half-time show is to know his customer, the audience. He knows what they *expect,* and he knows what they *don't expect,* so he gives them some of both.

That's exactly the same strategy I think we have to use in a selling situation or in a job interview.

For a half-time spectacle, what's expected is a zillion bands, a zillion dancers on platforms, and a laser light show. For a job interview, it's being on time, dressing appropriately, answering questions clearly and honestly, and being qualified.

But the part most people ignore, the part that makes the difference between getting the job and being an also-ran, is giving the interviewer what he or she doesn't expect. Be pleasingly unpredictable: Shock 'em. Don't be annoyingly erratic, be entertainingly original. For people like Lipton, who make their living creating this kind of event, it's the eighty-four pianos that he rolled out for the '84 Olympics in Los Angeles.

For you, it's the extra preparation and knowledge that can make you unforgettable at a job interview. One young person I was mentoring slam-dunked his interview with a major company by showing up toting his own slide show. Did that help the interviewers visualize him working for them? You bet.

You have to go the extra mile to produce that kind of *WOW* effect. You have to have more and better information than your fellow applicants have. You're not going to know about the company's recent on-time delivery problems with Tuscaloosa. But if you've gone to the bookstore and stocked up on the current buzzword books with the latest techniques for nailing down a job, the books that can get you through any rough patches in the road; if you've done your homework, gone to the business section of the library, and read every newspaper article, annual report, brokerage house analysis, Dun and Bradstreet; if you've talked to everyone you know who works for the company or who is a supplier or customer; quizzed your personal mentors, your advisers and instructors; if you've done all that, you're going to have a pretty good idea of the prospective company's current strategies, accomplishments, problems, and needs. And you're going to know how to demonstrate your ability to meet them and fit into the company groove.

You'll have a chance to use that information during your interview, and when you do, you will immediately have accomplished what few, if any, of your competitors have achieved. You will have put the *WOW* factor to work for you.

After I'd written my first book, *Swim with the Sharks,*

my publisher pulled out all the stops and booked me on "The Larry King Show." There I was, a total unknown, given a shot at what is undoubtedly one of the best author showcases in the country. King is heard nightly on 385 radio stations with an estimated audience of four million people.

It was do or die time. The book, and the years of work it represented, would succeed or fail based on what I did in the thirty minutes of air time I had been allotted with Larry King.

What to do now?

Memorize key passages from my book to recite?

Tell folks about the days of excitement and nights of intrigue that are the hallmarks of the envelope game? Try to recreate old Marx Brothers routines for a radio audience? See how many different color combinations I could wear at the same time and hope Larry would describe them on the air?

Instead, I decided to put into practice everything I'd been preaching about preparedness. I did a Mackay 66, the 66-question customer profile I describe in *Sharks*, on King himself. I read and reread his book *Tell It to the King*. I went digging around in the newspaper files at the library; I plundered *Who's Who*. I called his secretary. From what I'd learned about him from these sources, I called friends of his across the country for every scrap of information, professional and personal, I could find out about him.

I hired a local DJ (who thought I was nuts, but who went along with the gag for an appropriate honorarium) to conduct mock interviews where he played King to my commoner.

Then, I listened to King every night for eighteen straight nights until my scheduled appearance.

I knew his moves.

Finally, it was showtime.

As luck would have it, almost at the top of the show, a caller asked me a question that triggered a story I'd recently read about Arthur Godfrey, an enormously successful radio personality in his day and a master pitchman. Godfrey was filling out a driver's license application and when he came to the question of occupation, he didn't hesitate to emphasize the side of his personality that had buttered his bread for so many years. He put down "salesman." Thus ended any mystery as to why Arthur Godfrey had been able to enjoy such a long and successful show business career. He knew how to keep sponsors, as well as audiences, happy.

Having made my point about that, I then said, "You'll find that story in a highly readable, very useful book I recently read called *Tell It to the King,* by one Larry King."

King's jaw dropped to his knees, a grin spread over his face, he snapped his famous suspenders, and we settled down to a two-hour on-the-air session, four times the length of the originally scheduled segment.

From that point on, thanks to Larry King, *Sharks* swam right to the top of the charts.

18

IF YOU WANT TO BE HEARD, TRY TURNING UP THE VOLUME

Last year in Pittsburgh a radio talk show altered its format from the usual rantings about abortion and gun control to let the jobless and unemployed read their resumes over the air. The gimmick generated about forty calls from potential employers.

For those who have tried everything else, including offering their services through the classified sections of the newspaper, why not try advertising on the radio, particularly if you're looking for a job in a creative business like advertising or publishing? Use a blind post office box for a reply to avoid the loonies, and keep it light and clever. Why pound the pavement when you can call in an airstrike?

19

**SOMETIMES IT PAYS
TO THINK SMALL**

In thirty-one years of hiring good people, one of the main problems I have had is cutting through the fog of misinformation that seems to engulf most first-time job seekers. When young people come out of school, they especially love to hit the biggies, the Fortune 500 companies—Procter & Gamble, General Electric, IBM. That's where they think the action is, that's where the growth is, and the game plan is to start at the top and work your way up.

Although many big companies are still excellent places to work, that strategy has sidetracked more promising careers than doing killer imitations of the boss at the office Christmas party. To begin with, since 1980 the Fortune 500 companies have lost 4.4 million jobs. The real growth in the economy is found in the small to medium-sized companies, where you can also get more hands-on job training, plus less corporate red tape and a greater chance for advancement. It's the monster-sized companies that have a meeting to see if they should have a meeting.

The smaller outfits are also more likely to act fast in terms of new ideas and techniques. For decades, IBM used to let the little guys generate the new products and then wait for them to overextend themselves on service or performance. Then IBM would sweep in with second-generation products that had the bugs worked out and use their superior marketing and financial muscle to pick up the business. The saying used to be that "no one ever got fired for specifying IBM."

It doesn't work that way anymore. It's the IBMs that are shrinking, trying to dismantle their giant bureaucracies and boutique their businesses in order to provide quicker responses to customer needs. They let the little guys get too far ahead in both pricing and technology. Now they're playing catch-up.

Don't forget to think small, because that's where a lot of the big opportunities are. If job seekers only realized that there are thousands of growing, dynamic smaller companies within a stone's throw of where they live, they wouldn't concentrate all their firepower on the same ones everyone else is aiming at.

In my own metropolitan area, with a mere population of 2.3 million, there are 76,000 small businesses within a sixty-minute driving radius. Many of these places are run and owned by entrepreneurs, people who couldn't or wouldn't fit into the corporate mold, saw a niche in the marketplace, and had the energy and nerve to go out on their own. These people tend to be more intuitive operators than by-the-numbers types, and more willing to try new ideas, new approaches, and new people.

And because these smaller outfits usually don't see as many applicants, the barriers to entry tend to be easier to overcome than the barriers to entry at big companies.

Have I mentioned that small companies offer the better chance to get a job? Let me put it another way: Small entrepreneurial companies offer you the better chance to get rich, too.

One out of every two hundred people in the United States is a millionaire, making us a nation of a million millionaires. With a million different ways to make your pile grow to a million bucks, one of the toughest is always going to be working for wages at a big company.

Another way you should think small is in terms of location. If what you do is more important to you than where you do it, don't get sucked into the San Francisco Syndrome. There will always be a tight job market in the glamour spots, and you'll always pay more for the privilege of living there.

Think in terms of smaller towns within striking distance of your dream city, or bigger towns that are somehow flawed in the public mind, like the Twin Cities, with a reputation for bad weather. (They cry when they come … but they cry when they leave.) They'll offer you a lot more job choices and, once you get in the swim, you'll find every cultural asset or lifestyle element that's available anywhere else. The difference between most bigger cities and most smaller ones is usually not a matter of finding a version of what you're looking for, it's that once you find it, the subvarieties can run a little thin. Everything's there, but often there's only one of a kind.

If you can handle that, you won't need a San Francisco to satisfy your personal needs.

One other consideration: Smaller company/smaller town equals less chance of forced relocation. It's up to you whether that's a plus or a minus on your personal scorecard.

Any way you add it up, avoid the crowds. A job search is not a group activity. Don't think that because all the fishermen are clustered around one spot on the lake that that's where all the fish are going to be. Bass are where you find them. More jobs are uncovered by using the right bait at the right depth in the right waters than by simply throwing in your line with the rest of the crowd.

20

TRUST YOUR FIRST IMPRESSIONS INSTEAD OF YOUR SECOND THOUGHTS

If all human responses were rational and predictable, I suppose we'd complain about the boredom instead of the frustration. At least that's how I comfort myself when faced for the quadrillionth time with one of life's little lunacies. The one I'm referring to is what I call the cocktail party factor. I come within an eyelash of closing a deal or getting a commitment only to see the whole thing unravel for totally illogical reasons.

I interview and interview and finally everything clicks. I find a person I want to hire. Just as important, the feeling is mutual. The prospective employee is equally eager to go to work for us.

Then something happens.

I get a call the next day. The prospect has cooled off. He or she will give me a reason, but we both know it's a phony one. The given reason is *never* the real reason. If I had been a fly on the wall when my hot prospect went home that evening, I'd bet the conversation went something like this:

"Honey, guess what? I got a job."

"That's wonderful. I'm so proud of you. What is it?"

"Well, I'm selling envelopes."

"Oh."

"You know, envelopes. Those things we get our bills in, what we use to send out our Christmas cards."

"Yes, I know."

The spouse has instantly flashed to their next social gathering, to the moment where she or he reports that The Unemployed One has landed a job. Finally.

Selling envelopes.

Demeaning. Sad. Degrading. Second-class citizen.

They just can't handle it.

That's what drives so many people to the Procter & Gambles of the world.

Where they earn *less* money.

Selling soap.

But at least they can say they work for Procter & Gamble.

The *National Business Employment Weekly* has a name for it: "job snobs." Is that attitude keeping you from going to work for a small, obscure local company or one of the less ritzy national biggies like Wal-Mart or Pizza Hut? Did you know that "salaries for fast-food and retail assistant store managers start in the low to mid-twenties," and that "managers often make $40,000 a year"? says the *National Business Employment Weekly*.

Don't be like Chester, the guy who made his living at the circus cleaning up after the elephants.

An old friend saw him one day and said, "My God, Chester, what's become of you? You have to get out of here and get yourself a decent job."

"What, and quit show business?"

21

HELP WANTED
PLEEEEEEEEEEEEEEEEEEEEEZE

The envelope business is hardly the only target of the cocktail party mindset.

I'm holding two newspaper clippings. One headline, from the *Miami Herald,* reads, "Car Dealers Puzzled by Lack of Job Applicants." The other headline, from the *Naples* (Florida) *Daily News* is, "Young People Don't Want to Become Toolmakers."

Two perfectly respectable jobs, one white-collar, one blue-collar, both going begging. What gives?

It can't be the pay. I know of kids right out of college who've earned forty thousand dollars their first year selling cars, exactly the figure that appears in the *Herald.* I thought it was tough getting car buyers into the show-rooms. Now you can't even get salespeople. Not even the promise of a five thousand-dollar sign-up bonus has been able to attract job applicants (and I thought only guys with ninety-mile-an-hour fastballs got bonuses).

As for machinists in the Midwest, although the average pay is $32,000 to $36,000 a year, young workers aren't signing up for the training programs. Nationwide, the number of people enrolled in apprentice programs has dipped 61 percent since 1986. When you consider all skilled blue-collar trades, according to the Congressional Office of Technology Assessment, the United States is near the bottom in comparison with other industrialized countries in the percentage of workers who have completed apprenticeship programs. For instance, in Germany, the figure is 6.5 percent. In the United States, it's .16 percent. The decimal point *is* in the right place, representing one-sixth of 1 percent of our workforce, a percentage which is 1/40th that of Germany.

I can appreciate why the chance to flip burgers at a fast food joint may not set hearts aflutter, but honestly, does the world really need any more actors, stockbrokers, investment bankers, journalists, and lawyers?

A woman called a plumber to come out to her house. Just as her husband arrived home he sees her paying the plumber ninety dollars for just a few minutes of work. "That's ridiculous," the husband fumed. "I'm a lawyer and I don't even charge that much!"

"I know," the plumber answered. "That's why I got out of law!"

It doesn't hurt to look into some of the less glamorous areas, particularly sales and skilled trades.

What they may lack in panache they could make up in cash.

22

YOU CAN PUT A NEW SPIN
ON AN OLD
RACQUET

Last winter I was at the John Gardiner Tennis Ranch in Phoenix. I've played tennis most of my life, but I'm still not as good as I want to be. So I go to camps. I read books. I watch videotapes. I take lessons. I watch great players play. I do everything I can to continue to improve.

One morning I signed up to play a doubles match. The way it works is that when four people show up, partners are decided by spinning a racquet. When I got to the court, the others were already there and one of the fellows was visibly upset. It seems he didn't want to be paired with a certain party who happened to be ninety years old. No spin-the-racquet today. He wasn't taking any chances.

I usually don't have any particular preference about partners, but I had a hunch about this one, so I agreed to take the ninety-year-old wallflower to the dance.

The first two sets, we hammered our opponents 6-1, 6-1. My partner barely twitched a muscle. He could put the ball anywhere he wanted and, to top it off, came in behind his serve. As we were switching sides to play the third set, he said to me: "Do you mind if I play the backhand court? I always like to work on my weaknesses." You bet. I've always believed in the proposition that you never stop learning, but this guy tended to carry things to extremes. A member of his college tennis team, class of '22, the year before Warren Harding died in office, this gentleman was still doing postgraduate work nearly seventy years later. The score of the third set was also 6-1.

As we walked off the court that day, my ninety-year-old partner said to me, "I thought you might like to know that I am ranked number one in the United States in my age bracket, the eighty-five years old and up group."

He wasn't thinking, "ninety." He wasn't even thinking, "eighty-five, and hey, I can beat guys seventy-five and younger." No, he was thinking, "Number one. I'm number one. And it's going to take a lot of time and practice, but I'm going to work my butt off to stay number one."

This man is every employer's dream. Age is not a consideration. He is a hungry fighter. He doesn't know it, but he is *my* hero.

A few months later I met his soulmate in a New York taxicab. In my opinion, a ride in a New York cab is about as much fun as a tax audit, except that the IRS guy is usually more likeable than your average New York City cab driver. The cabs are always filthy, the bulletproof partition makes you feel like you're being hauled off to Sing Sing, and the drivers act like they just got released from there. Their motto is: "Politeness is a sign of weakness."

Not this cab. It was sparkling clean. There was beautiful music coming out of the sound system and, believe it or not, no bulletproof partition. My driver had taken the great leap of faith and concluded that not everybody was out to mug him.

I said to the driver, "LaGuardia Airport, please." He turned around, smiled, and said, "Hi, my name is Wally." And he handed me a piece of paper. At the top it said, "Mission Statement." That's right, Mission Statement! It said he was going to get me where I was going safely, courteously, and on time.

As he pulled away from the curb, he held up copies of the *New York Times* and *USA Today*.

"Be my guest," said Wally.

A few minutes into the ride he motioned to me not to be bashful and to help myself to some of the fruit in the basket on the backseat. Then he asked me if I preferred to listen to another kind of music, perhaps rock and roll, from his audio tape collection. Classical, Wally's original choice, suited me just fine.

About ten minutes later, he held up a cellular phone and said, "Would you like to make a call? I have to charge for this one. It's a dollar a minute."

I couldn't control myself any longer. "Where did you learn this?" I asked.

"On a talk show."

"How long have you been doing it?"

"Three, four years."

"Look, I know this is prying, but do you mind sharing something with me? How much extra money do you earn in tips because of the way you run your business here?"

"You IRS?"

"No, Wally."

"I figure ten, maybe twelve thou a year."

Wally, a graduate of no school, never stopped learning either. He's even more of an ideal employee than Mr. Number One Tennis Player. Wally proved there are no such things as dead-end jobs, only deadheads at jobs. He's living proof that you can shift the odds in your favor, find the bass where no one else is looking, if you apply some market savvy and imagination and give the customers what no one else is willing to give them. Wally won't be driving a cab forever, unless he wants to. My guess is that if I ever land in a Wally-like cab in New York again, the driver will be working for Wally.

There's a classic story on the subject.

Homer, a shoe salesman, is sent to the deepest, darkest jungles of equatorial Africa. Pretty soon, he wires back to the home office, "They don't wear shoes here. No one's buying. Ship me home. Homer."

So they do.

The company decides to give it one more shot, so they pack off superstar Rodney, their best salesman, to Africa. In one week, a telegram comes back, "Start shipping shoes immediately … no competition here! Rodney."

No matter how tough times get, there are never enough Rodneys.

23

LADIES AND GENTLEMEN ... REV UP
YOUR RESUMES

Business is an imperfect, imprecise form of human activity. Too many managers think that when a business gets in trouble all they need to do is reach for the numbers, knock them around a little, and both the cause and the solution to the problem will leap magically off the spreadsheet and grab them by the lapels.

"Okay, if we just fix this one itty-bitty little thing, everything's going to be all better, real soon."

In your dreams, pal.

When something is wrong enough to cause the numbers to hemorrhage, usually lots of things have gone wrong from product, manufacturing, pricing, marketing, financing, personnel, organization … to you yourself.

Best answer: all of the above.

You won't need a microscope to find what you're looking for. It's found you. You'll have to plug many, many leaks in the dike to keep from drowning in red ink.

Job finding is also an imperfect, imprecise form of human activity. You can do dozens of things right and find you're also doing dozens of things wrong. Networking, creative resumes, pounding the pavement, attending seminars, making new contacts, keeping in shape, mentally, physically, sartorially. You have to do them all at once, and all of them correctly, in order to reach your goal. It's folly to rely on one strategy or one strong point and ignore the other links in the chain.

Resumes are one of those links, though I tend to believe they're not much help in picking a candidate. As Stanley Randall said, "The closest to perfection a person ever comes is when he fills out a job application form." In my experience, they're so predictably inflated you might as well pick a spouse sight unseen from the wondrous descriptions in the personals column. Hard to believe there are that many lonely, young, gorgeous, brilliant, wealthy people in the world craving my companionship and my tired old body.

But then, if they were not sight unseen, at least you'd be able to know what they're bragging about.

So why not attach a picture of yourself to your resume? I may not like resumes much, but I'm usually a sucker for a new approach. Out of the last fifty resumes I've seen, not a single one had a photo included.

I think I know why. There are very reasonable concerns about "lookism" and discrimination. If everyone sent in a photo with their application, the pretty face, by our culture's movie star definition of pretty, would stand the best chance of being interviewed and eventually hired.

Minorities, people with disabilities, people who for various superficial reasons don't meet our pop culture standards for personal appearance, would be at a disadvantage.

I think that's true in our society, and I also think it's a terrible thing that it is true. If you believe it's happened to you, if you can prove discrimination and have a legal basis for a lawsuit, then let them have it with both barrels.

But, if anyone is ever going to hire you, whether they're good guys or bad guys, they've got to see you *sometime*. You can't show up for the interview or for work with a bag over your head, so why not at least give the potential employer a chance to attach a face to a name and send in a photo with your application? They will never *ask* you to do that, of course, because then they're making themselves vulnerable to charges of discrimination, but if you do it voluntarily, I guarantee you one thing, you're going to stand out from the crowd ... and that's one way to get a foot in the door.

Another way to distinguish your resume visually from the crowd is to hire a professional graphic designer to lay it out for you. Have it done conservatively. No glaring colors or weird typefaces. It'll cost you a little, but when 99 out of 100 resumes seem to look and read like they were banged out on the same word processor by the same person, you'll stand out. You're wearing the drop-dead suit. They're wearing torn jeans. In a world where first impressions matter, a well-designed resume is your chance to make a good one.

Every resume and job application form asks you to list references. You've anticipated that, of course. You have several old standbys you've trotted out for years, on the assumption that once having promised you, many, many moons ago, they always would say nice things about you if called upon to do so, that their promise was undying and eternal. Maybe. Maybe not.

Sure, you've exchanged Christmas cards every year (or, wait a minute, do you remember actually *seeing* their card, or is it possible you didn't make the cut in the last year or two?).

Add three things to the list of life's little certainties: One, nothing is forever; two, potential employers, anxiously taking every possible precaution to protect themselves from bad hires, really do check references; and three, you can't take anything for granted.

Get my drift? It's time to freshen up those crucially important references just in case there's a loose cannon somewhere on deck.

Imagine a prospective employer calling a key reference who is "forced" to confess, "Honestly, when Cheryl worked here years ago, it was more as a junior gofer than as a junior auditor. But, hey, I never had a brighter, more eager, more enthusiastic entry-level employee, even though we finally had to let her go ... Why? ... Well, she was really good at what she did and she always wanted more responsibility, but she didn't get along with the other people in the department very well, though I bet she's a lot better at that sort of thing now."

Not exactly a rave review, is it? And, of course, you'll never get a true answer from your reference as to what he or she said in your behalf.

But if you keep scoring aces on your interviews only to find that you never make the traveling squad, you better check out the basics.

Take a reference to lunch. Take them all to lunch, one at a time.

Many people are literally afraid of tampering with a good reference for fear of harming the *Wunderkind* impression they made earlier in their careers. Wrongo. You won't blow it with the touchy/feely thing, and by keeping them informed of your progress, it's the best fire insurance you can buy. Besides, good references can also be good friends and valuable mentors. Just remember: As in all cases where you're trying to keep up your contacts, care and feeding are required.

24

HOW I GOT THE JOB I WANTED, #3

This was the day, and that old gospel hymn, "Keep Your Eye on the Prize," was in my head. I was determined to find and land a job that jumped my salary up a few notches. I was going to get on a promising career path and do some fast walking.

The sun came through the kitchen curtains and I had settled into my second cup of Sunday morning coffee. From a page of ads, one caught my eye. Bordered in black, it read something like this:

Director—National health association seeks director/manager with established track record. Will operate membership services, work with student representatives, plan national convention. Excellent salary, benefits, surroundings, growth potential, for a person with the right experience.

This was perfect: a key administrative position in the health care field, an area that was growing quickly. My task was obvious. To land the job, I first had to get an interview. And given my lack of background in health, the competition from experienced health professionals would be rough.

Further, I had never worked for an association and didn't know anything about how they operated. Membership services? I drew a blank. Organizing a convention? No experience. My track record was excellent. But most of my professional experience had been as director of student activities at a university. I was currently serving as director of a small foundation. So that was what I had to bring them: experience as a director and experience working with students.

To apply for this job, I took out my resume and reread it. I stopped by the library and picked up recent articles on issues in American health care and service delivery. I then *rewrote* the resume, making every possible connection to the field of health, to working with students, to membership organizations and services, and to meeting and convention planning.

My stated objective: Top leadership position in a health-related organization or membership organization. In the resume and the letter I talked about the challenge facing the American health care system and the opportunities that attracted me to it.

My leadership experience: I emphasized working closely with student membership organizations including clubs and fraternities.

My convention planning experience: I referred to the responsibilities of the Student Activities office for scheduling student meetings and conferences.

My references: All three I listed with my application were physicians.

Finally, I followed all the standard rules: Keep the resume short and tight with no typos or other errors, make sure it is attractively laid out and typed and is on high-quality paper.

A month later I had the job. I received a 50 percent boost in pay, a lovely office, a several-person staff, and a very pleasant work environment. Further, when I was hired, they told me that they only interviewed two candidates. And I was told my resume was by far the best they received.

Assume there are 100–150 resumes submitted for the position. How much time do you think will be spent looking at each one? My guess is that 90 percent will receive twenty seconds or less. Of the others, I'd guess two or three minutes is spent, at the most. The best resumes—those of the "sure thing" interviewees— may be initially looked at for only ten seconds and then put on the small "yes" pile. Why? Because they have direct, high-quality experience at a very similar job. This is where I wanted my resume to be. And it was.

Ironically, given my excellent resume, all my interviewer had to do was confirm in person what I'd said in writing: I was an excellent person for the job.

If this story has a moral, it is simply do what the

hymn says. Don't lose sight of the prize. Most people writing resumes are thinking about themselves. In doing so, they forget about the job for which they are applying. They express an interest in a "challenging job with opportunities for growth." Sometimes the resume says that the person is willing to work in business *or* education *or* in a not-for-profit organization. Their resumes are vague. The person reviewing applications then looks at this and sees a mishmash.

Use the language of the ad whenever possible to describe what you have done. Never falsify, but emphasize those parts of your experience that will get you in for an interview. When interviewed, your task is then simply to show the interviewer that you are just as good as, or better than, the resume indicates.

Remember, for you, the prize is the job. But for your future employer, the prize is you.

D.B. Lamb
Chicago, Illinois

25

ONE SIZE DOES NOT FIT ALL

One common bit of job-hunting advice is the Publisher's Clearing House–type approach: market saturation. The theory is, you can't catch a fish unless your bait is in the water, so the more bait you throw in, the more chances you have to land a bass.

People have told me they have mailed out a hundred, five hundred, a thousand resumes, and maybe it works, but the next sentence after the one where they wow me with the number is, "and I didn't get a single nibble."

I suspect the reason is that when you send out a thousand resumes, anyone who gets one can look at it and see immediately you sent out the exact same thing to 999 other potential employers. You have to customize. You have to go after your target with a rifle shot and not with carpet bombing. After all, whatever job you're after is one of a kind. Potential employers are looking for a special person with special qualities. If *they* don't feel that every one of the thousand people who apply is fit for the position, why should *you* expect that if you send out exactly the same resume to a thousand potential employers, there is any special reason for them to want to hire you?

There's just no substitute for doing your homework and making your approach fit the individual you're pitching.

Years ago Toots Shor ran a restaurant in New York City which, unlike most world-famous restaurants, really was world-famous. One day, he flew back into town, jumped into a cab, and, posing as a naïve tourist, said to the driver, "This is my first time in New York. I'd like to go to a wonderful restaurant. Any suggestions?"

The cabbie said, "Oh yes! For years I've been recommending Toots Shor's restaurant to all my passengers. It's got marvelous food, drink, atmosphere, ambience."

Shor beamed with pride.

Forty minutes later the cab pulled up in front of the restaurant, with the driver still holding forth on the garden of earthly delights to be found in Shor's saloon. Shor got out, pulled out a hundred-dollar bill, and handed it to the driver. "Keep the change, cabbie," he said.

"Gee," said the driver, "thanks a lot, Mr. Shor."

That's what I mean by tailor-making your pitch to fit the audience.

26

KNOW THYSELF TO GET THYSELF HIRED

Recently, major league sports have added a new spectacle to the events calendar: Draft Day. It's a miracle of modern promotion. Sports events used to feature sports. Now, the fantasy element has become equally huge, and fans gather by the thousands in local sports arenas to watch TV coverage of middle-aged men in suits fumbling with ping pong balls, making solemn-sounding announcements and scribbling on blackboards. Who's getting who? Who's trading? Who's standing pat? Who's expendable? Who's untouchable? What kind of talent is in demand, in decline? Who got snookered, who snatched a prize from under everybody else's nose? Who's winning, who's losing? No one really knows, because you can't score a contest where no one gets the ball until next year, but it's a great game for any fan who gets off on lots of controversy and strongly held expressions of opinion.

Most of the Draft Day hype and hope focuses on athletic skills, but sophisticated general managers, who are responsible for these multimillion-dollar decisions, know they have to factor in other elements. They realize that the performance of their choices will depend as much on their personal qualities as on their raw physical talent. Stats are for fans. Rosters are filled with players whose stats conceal their real value. George Steinbrenner and Gene Autry, consummate amateurs, always manage to come up with rosters of awe-inspiring paper power ... and cost ... but can't build teams with the kind of chemistry that wins pennants.

It's little wonder. Personal qualities are a lot tougher to get a handle on than the numbers for the forty-yard dash or the vertical jump. Is this player committed? What is his value system? Is he coachable? Will he be a team player? Will he be able to overcome his shortcomings? Will he choke? Does he quit? Has he established sound training habits?

Sports franchises are built on the answers to these kinds of questions.

So are businesses.

For thirty years, I have relied on industrial psychologists to help me sort out the complexities of a hire. According to the American Management Association, about one in five companies in the United States is now using psychological testing, and the trend is growing rapidly.

Fortunately for us business types, it's a lot easier to get your subject to test when he's a forty-five-year-old salesperson than a nineteen-year-old athlete ... even though with the athlete you may be risking ten million dollars or more on the results. Just imagine the fan reaction if you were able to get one of these kids to test for you and you came up with something like "We decided not to draft Mr. All-American because, even though he can shoot the eyes out of the basket from forty feet, he has an unresolved conflict with authority figures."

Whatever the results, I never let the industrial psychologists make the decision for me. Their information is just another tool in the hiring process.

But it's a tool you can use to your own advantage as a prospective employee.

In two ways.

If you suddenly find yourself scanning the horizons for a job, I recommend you get yourself to an industrial psychologist and get tested. On your own.

I'm not going to kid you, it's not cheap. It will cost you four to five hundred dollars, but the oral and written exams will uncover strengths you never dreamed you had (and a few weaknesses to work on also). If you're being let go, try to talk your employer into paying the tab as part of your outplacement package.

Remember, you're at a crossroads in your life, and the next job you take could determine your future for a long time to come. Isn't it worth your while to know whether you're heading in the right direction? If there was ever a time to change careers, to rethink your goals, isn't this it? Fate has forced you into this situation, so take advantage of it, play out the hand you've been dealt, and find out about yourself and what you're good at. Don't do it on the cheap. Go to a firm with an excellent reputation, so you know you're getting a sound evaluation from someone who's a lot less biased about you than you are.

Arthur Rubinstein witnessed a car accident and was called into court to testify. On the witness stand he was asked his name. "My name is Arthur Rubinstein." He was then asked his occupation and he stated, "I am the world's greatest pianist." After he stepped down from testifying and was on his way out of the courthouse, a cub reporter rushed up to him and said, "Mr. Rubinstein, don't you think that was a little presumptuous the way you described yourself back there?" "But my son, what could I do, I was under oath?"

Not all of us have such a clear picture of our own skills and using a psychologist to fill in the blanks doesn't seem so expensive if it tells you some things about yourself that can be of permanent benefit to you.

Another use is this: You now have in your hands the kind of report that 99.9 percent of other job seekers—your competitors—don't have. It contains information every interviewer is trying to learn about a prospect before they commit the company to a hire. Armed with this psychological profile, you now have your own personal Good Housekeeping Seal of Approval, a way of providing potential employers with the valuable information they want.

Does it show that you are a less than perfect human being? Of course. Not to worry. We all are. What it also shows is that you have areas of strength, as well as creativity and imagination in your job-seeking skills. And that may be just enough to resolve the decision in your favor.

Rice University, the doormat of the Southwest Conference in football, has always been the grade point average leader, the toughest school academically in this all-Texas conference. Years ago, someone told me about an alleged cheer of theirs. They call it the "existential cheer." I've always gotten a kick out it and kept it on a three-by-five card, wondering if I'd ever find a place to use it. Well, this is the place:

We're from Rice.
Ain't that nice?
Who are you?
Do you know?

It will pay you to find out.

27

IT DOESN'T HURT TO KNOW
THE OTHER GUY EITHER

On a steaming 100 degree day at the 1992 Summer Olympic Games in Barcelona, Spain, I found myself jammed into a crowd waiting to enter the women's gymnastics event. Nothing visible but heads and armpits in every direction. Suddenly, eight feet above the masses, rose a huge sign. On it in big block letters was written, "I need tickets" in not one, but *ten* languages.

As the crowd began to move, I elbowed my way over to the sign bearer, a Spaniard, and asked him how his marketing device was working. "I haven't missed an event yet."

The average Spaniard or American doesn't typically know ten languages. But we can find out. That's doing your homework and knowing your audience.

If you're applying for a job at Mackay Envelope, before you see the inside of our plant, be resourceful and visit another operation first. Take a tour of duty with an envelope salesperson. Phone the Envelope Manufacturers Association of America and have them mail you a few copies of the trade publication and the latest propaganda on the issues facing the industry. Go to the post office. Go to a big direct mailer. They handle our products every day and they'll tell you how envelopes are used, which ones work for one purpose, which ones for another. All envelopes are not created equal.

Neither are all job candidates. Of the five hundred or so I've interviewed personally, only one has ever done this.

If I wanted to break into the training program at Pepsi, one thing I'd do would be to go and find out everything I could about Coke. I'd talk to mass marketers and small retailers, soda pop outlets and restaurants, read everything I could lay my hands on from the bookstores, libraries, and brokerage offices, and then write a major report on the competition's principal weaknesses together with my comments, analysis, constructive suggestions, and questions.

Every business, no matter how successful, needs fresh insights into its problems, and the more well run the business, the more likely it is to be open to creative approaches.

I'd hand-carry or express my thesis to the person doing the hiring, and if that didn't get me an interview, I'd update my report three months later and send it off again, and keep doing it until that crack in the door finally appeared. Chances are, it will.

This exercise quickly propels you to the short list when and if they are hiring.

28

IF YOU'RE AS WONDERFULLY HAPPY, COMPETENT, WELL-QUALIFIED, AND SUCCESSFUL AS IT SAYS HERE IN THIS RESUME, WHY ARE YOU SITTING ACROSS FROM ME NOW LOOKING FOR A JOB?

Having never received a credible answer to that question, I long ago stopped believing resumes. In fact, just about the first question I ask a job applicant is: "What are your greatest weaknesses?" Talk about *WOW*. You should hear the answers to that one. "I'm too honest." "I'm a workaholic." My favorite is "I don't think I've ever been able to stop thinking envelopes, envelopes, envelopes."

This from a forty-three-year-old salesperson, and a pretty good one, who never sold an envelope before in his life. I wonder why it took him so long to try and satisfy this all-embracing lifetime obsession.

The point is, of course, no employer ever read a bad resume, so don't lay it on too thick, either on paper or during the job interview. Sure, you've got weaknesses and problems. You're human, aren't you? Maybe you find it tough to take orders. Maybe sometimes you have trouble rolling out of bed in the morning and making it to work on time. Maybe you don't handle criticism very well and on your last job you felt you had more than your share. Maybe you hate to file written reports or fill out forms. I certainly have been told enough times, after a view of my office, I should consider joining the local chapter of Messies Anonymous, and it is a standing joke that to hand me an important piece of paper of any kind is to guarantee its disappearance quicker than washers and dryers can swallow up dirty socks.

If I were you, I wouldn't advertise it, but I'd sure admit to less than perfection, particularly if you are asked directly and it was a cause, or a contributing factor, in your leaving your last job. And I'd follow up with a strong defense as to *why* it happened and how you intend to deal with the situation in the future. Chances are, you stand a better shot of getting and holding a new job if you're up-front under questioning than if you lie or attempt a water-walking act at your job interview.

Now that you've just read this, let me reach across the pages for a moment and try to deal with that skeptical expression I see planted on your face. "Yeah, it's easy for him to say," you're thinking. "He's not out there on the pavement competing with 150 other people for the same job, all of them lying their pants off about how perfect they are. No one's going to hire me if I have a hair out of place, much less if I come across as some kind of reformed ax murderer."

Okay, you've got a point. I don't really buy it, but let me make a suggestion that's going to make it easier for you to deal with the kind of tough questions that can come up in a job interview.

Hold a practice session. Have your friends help you work on your interviewing skills using the techniques described in the next few chapters, so you're confident and prepared to go into battle.

Did you know that every good lawyer who's arguing a case on appeal always sets aside a day or two for rehearsals, where other lawyers ask the kinds of probing questions the judges are likely to ask when the case is actually argued? Why? Because both sides in any lawsuit usually have some pretty strong points in their favor or the case wouldn't be appealed. And, of course, one side's strength is the other side's weakness.

Before Notre Dame plays at Tennessee, in the noisiest stadium in the country, Lou Holtz prepares his team by playing crowd noise at unbearably loud levels throughout the entire week of practice.

It doesn't take much of a stretch of the imagination to realize that as a job applicant, you're like the lawyer arguing a case on appeal to a judge or like the coach preparing to perform under tough conditions.

Or like the worker who opens up a lunch pail and sees it's bologna sandwiches. He goes into a tirade. "Nuts! Bologna sandwiches yesterday, bologna sandwiches the day before, bologna sandwiches today." His friend interrupts and says, "Relax, just tell your wife to make you another kind." "Are you kidding, I made them myself!"

The Bible tells us to love our enemies, and not many of us do, but it's really pretty good advice. Especially when the enemy is *us*. Unless we come to grips with our weaknesses, even if they are never touched upon in a job interview, they can always come back to haunt us when we're the most vulnerable. So face them squarely. It could be vital to your getting a job, and from your own point of view, it's a first step toward correcting them.

Now, if you'll just excuse me for a moment, I have to straighten out my desk. I seem to have misplaced my notes for the next chapter ...

29

EXPOSE YOURSELF IN THE PRIVACY OF YOUR OWN HOME

On to that practice session I just mentioned. Let's do the job right.

Do you remember how, just before your boss "lost confidence in you," and set your rear end on the cobblestones, you and your mate bought that $699 video camera at the discount electronic store? You may have bought it to take memorable pictures of little Johnnie sucking his thumb, but why not use it to make adult videos? No, not the X-rated kind—the kind that can help you find a job.

These days, big-cigar executives everywhere take expensive video training courses to fine-tune their performances when they go before the media or give speeches.

Well, the most important pitch you're ever going to give is to your potential new boss. So let's put modern management science to work for you. We can't quite gear up to the level of a professional speech course, but it won't cost you fifteen hundred dollars either, and the experience can polish your approach in several significant ways. For this to be worthwhile, you need to keep some rules in mind.

1. First, you need two friends. I don't recommend asking either a spouse or a relative. Preferably your pals should be people your age and career level. It would be best if they're in the same business or profession, because you want people who have a good idea of what's really happening in the jungle these days, who can ask intelligent questions and critique how you come across.

2. One friend is the cameraperson. The other is the interviewer. No need for artsy effects or other attempts at Academy Award–winning camerawork. Just have the cameraperson focus on you—especially your expressions—and have the cameraperson stay as invisible as possible. The less you're aware of the camera, the better.

3. You're not playing it for laughs. Get all your stand-up shtick out of your system in the first five minutes, and get on with it. Your tape may be a tad light on production values, but this is serious stuff.

4. Make sure the interviewer is thoroughly briefed on the firm he is supposed to be representing. You should know—so your pal can be an effective questioner—about the firm's business reputation, what their hot buttons and idiosyncrasies are, how they do business. Tell the interviewer what kinds of questions you expect will be toughest for you to answer, but don't put the exact words in his mouth. You want that mock interviewer to be a tough, believable, serious questioner ... just what you would expect from the real thing. Ideally, give the interviewer a

list of questions you've encountered before in actual interviews so he or she can rework them in their own style. (See The Mackay 22, chapter 33.)

5. This is not a performance. They have already cast all the roles in *Sons of Young Guns III*. Don't ever memorize an answer to a question. You want spontaneity. The last thing you need is to come off like the person on the dance floor who obviously just completed the three thousand-dollar Golden Lifetime course of rumba lessons. Canned responses are as undisguisable and unpersuasive as canned laughter on a sit-com rerun.

6. Try to be brief and to the point.

7. If the questions are penetrating and well asked, there will be moments when you hesitate, tighten up, avert your eyes, or laugh something off. If the cameraperson has the skill and your equipment can zoom in on you when you do this, all the better. More than likely, you will not have been aware of your own nervous patterns. Now you are.

8. Tape about fifteen minutes or so. Then stop. Now you and the film crew should all take a look at the instant replay. Get your team's honest input. Where do you come across as real, enthusiastic, and competent? Where do you sound phony, windy, defensive, or awkward? Replay the tape a couple of times. If you can sit through the umpteenth rerun of Michael Jordan highlights, you should be able to bear watching yourself a few times, even if you miss the easy layup now and then, especially if it helps you land a job.

As you go through the replay, the questioner should start thinking of new and improved questions. You should start thinking of new and improved answers, such as ideas and experiences that you want to fit in smoothly on the next go around.

9. Do a second interview—this time a little longer one.

It might be better if the cameraperson and the interviewer were to switch roles. Or even if you were to switch roles with the interviewer, so you can see how someone else handles the toughies. After you've been at it an hour, call it quits. Your concentration will start to fade.

10. After your real interview is over, compare the questions that were asked with those you used during the dress rehearsal. Were there any big surprises? You bet. Did you clutch? If you haven't secured that job yet, you have just fine-tuned the script for your next practice session.

There isn't a major public speaker in America who doesn't regularly clock time in front of a video camera. It's as much a part of their preparation as daily practice is to a concert pianist.

You may even want to save those practice tapes. In twenty years, after you've snagged the job and moved up to CEO, you can put your feet up on the desk, flip on the VCR, and look back at those dazzling answers that got you your first break.

30

THE MOST IMPORTANT JOB
SKILL YOU CAN HAVE

There is always going to be a place in the world for those who can express themselves clearly, quickly, and persuasively in the mother tongue. We've all been using it since we were toddlers, but most of us still aren't comfortable or proficient in expressing our thoughts. Too bad. Because the difference between careers is often not the quality of our ideas but the quality of our ability to express them.

The one uniform disqualifying characteristic of failed job candidates is grammatical or spelling mistakes on a resume. The iron rule is that if you cannot prepare an error-free communication while trying to get the job, you're going to mess up on the job. One of the saddest sights for me is to see a laboriously produced, letter-perfect resume, and then pick up the envelope (yes, we always examine the envelopes, what do you expect?) and see it addressed to Mr. Mackey, MacKay, McKay, McKey, McCay, Mackie … and on and on. You don't have to be able to spell "potato" to figure out what happens at our outfit when a job applicant makes Dan Quayle look smart.

Words are the most powerful tools in our society. They determine whom we vote for, what we believe in, what we buy. They move us to love, to hate, even to sacrifice our lives.

When the ancient Greeks compared Pericles to Demosthenes, Pericles was perceptive enough to know the difference. "When Pericles speaks, the people say, 'How well he speaks.' When Demosthenes speaks, they say, 'Let us march.'"

Don't squeeze all the juice out of what you believe in with mind-numbing jargon. Don't hide behind language. Use it to press your case. Present the facts, but keep in mind that leadership and success lie beyond facts; they lie in the ability to persuade.

Speaking, literature, and motivational courses all can help you improve your ability to communicate effectively. Upgrading your communications skills is the surest way to open the door to a job or to jumpstart a stalled career.

In my case, my mother, who was a schoolteacher, got me started at the tender age of twelve. At that time my idea of vocabulary upgrade consisted of adding to the string of cuss words I could say without repeating myself. A colorful skill, but of limited value in mixed company and made use of only at great personal risk within the Mackay household.

My mother had a different idea. She sent in for a subscription for me to *Reader's Digest*. It was in *my very own name*. In real print. The only other thing I owned that had my name on it was my pair of mittens. I was quite proud to think that in some distant precinct where *Reader's Digest* kept its records, my name was enrolled as a genuine subscriber and reader. On the first of every month, I'd start bugging Fred, the mailman, about when "my" subscription would arrive, and when it finally did, I devoured it cover to cover, particularly the twenty-question "Word Power" test. And you know, it's as easy for you to get started on it now as it was for me then.

You may not enjoy the same reward my parents gave me. If I got a really good score on the test, my dad took me to see the St. Paul Saints baseball game at Lexington Park. Second prize was a bucket of golf balls at the driving range minutes from my house. You'll have to arrange for your own prize.

Maybe a job?

31

___

OVERCOMING YOUR SPEECH IMPEDIMENT

Okay, now you have the vocabulary of an Oxford don, but what good is it if you can't use it effectively?

I've read that the greatest fear most of us have is asking for a raise and the second greatest is speaking in public. We'll deal with number one in another chapter. Let's concentrate on number two right here.

There's a very simple and effective solution.

Join Toastmasters International.

My father pushed me over the cliff to join just after I graduated from college, and it changed my life. I doubt if I would have written these books if it hadn't been for Toastmasters, because years before I thought of putting this material into book form, I was whipping it into shape in speeches.

If you've heard me speak, you know that I invariably ask the audience, "How many of you have heard of Toastmasters?" Every time, 98 percent of the hands go up. Then I ask, "How many are members or past members?" And 96 percent of the hands go down.

Incredible. By my informal count, only 2 percent of my audiences have experienced Toastmasters firsthand. Toastmasters has 175,000 members worldwide. For the past twenty-five years membership has grown at a healthy 7 percent clip, but that percentage is tiny when you think of the people who could benefit but haven't joined.

What's holding you back? I've never met anyone who joined who didn't think it was super valuable to their career. The skills we learn by overcoming our terror of speaking in public carry over to every word we utter trying to motivate and persuade others. We gain self-esteem, self-confidence, assertiveness. This makes us better salespeople, better managers, better leaders ... and stand-out job candidates. "No matter how much work a man can do, no matter how engaging his personality may be, he will not advance far in business if he cannot work through others," said John Craig. And you can't work through others unless you can communicate with them effectively.

If I still haven't persuaded you to join, here's another idea. Start an in-house Toastmasters group at your company. I've been advising people to try this for the last ten years and it's been an unqualified success.

I feel so strongly about this that anyone who reads this book, who joins Toastmasters for a year and doesn't feel the experience was worthwhile, can write to me at Mackay Envelope, 2100 Elm Street Southeast, Minneapolis,

Minnesota 55414. Enclose your dues statement, and I will return your money.

There's one condition. If you do feel that way and decide to write to me, take a look at the letter just before you mail it, and ask yourself: "Could I have written as good a letter if I hadn't joined Toastmasters?"

32

THE TOUGHEST JOB INTERVIEW QUESTION

So many people looking for jobs think something mystical will occur. The gods will either smile down upon them or not, and there really isn't much we can do but wait for the phone to ring.

They act like Melvin, who went to church every day for years and would kneel down and pray, "Please, God, let me win the lottery." Same prayer, every day. He never asked for anything else. Suddenly, one day, as he knelt praying, there was a clap of thunder, a bolt of lightning, and Melvin leaped up and yelled, "God, God, is that you?" A voice came back, "Yes, Melvin. It's me."

"Oh, thank you, God," says Melvin, "I knew you

would hear my prayers. I knew you were going to let me win the lottery."

"Melvin, Melvin, do me a favor … meet me halfway. Buy a ticket."

Moral: You have to make things happen. You can't just stand around all day and pray you're going to get a job.

A friend of mine, a Boston recruiter, likes to ask this question, "Well, what did you DO today?" He tells me he eliminates more prospects on the basis of their answer to this one than any other question in his arsenal.

Think of the ways you can answer.

For example, there's: "After I dragged myself out of the sack, I flipped on 'I Dream of Jeannie' and 'Battlestar Galactica.' They were pretty good today. Remember how Jeannie got trapped in the bottle and couldn't get out? And the time the Battleship wandered into the astroid field and it looked like it was going to get blown apart by negative energy from ion-charged megaparticles? Were they ever lucky to get out alive!

"Then, I shuffled into the kitchen, and wolfed down a couple of Snickers. No calls on the answering machine. Boy, that's a bummer. So I caught up on my research. This article in *People* on "Studs" is really a hoot.

"I like to keep active, so I grouted some tile in the bathroom. After that I debated whether I should get my hair cut today or wait until the unemployment check comes on Thursday. Tinkered with my resume. A couple of more rewrites and it should be a winner. Then I called around for an hour or so until I was able to bum a ride over to your place. And here I am."

Or, you could answer Mr. Boston this way:

"Pretty routine day, I guess. Between seven and nine o'clock I jogged, showered, read the *Boston Globe* and the *Wall Street Journal,* scoped out the classifieds, and added some possibles to my list of prospects for the phone calls I'd make today. Between nine and eleven, I worked on my files and met my quota of making five renewed contacts a day. Between calls, I knocked off a couple of follow-up and thank-you letters on my PC.

"By then, it was getting near lunchtime, so I threw some yogurt into a brown bag, headed down to the public library, logged forty-five minutes on trade journals to keep me fresh, and a half-hour to review some files in the business department on your company, Mr. Interviewer. And here I am."

We all know which answer you'd never give and the one you'd like to. The question is "*Which way do you really spend your time?*" And which lifestyle has the best chance of getting you back to work?

33

THE MACKAY 22

After an interview, do you know what happens in the office of the recruiter, personnel manager, or boss you just visited? It goes like this:

The manager closes the door. Opens the center drawer. Takes out an evaluation form. Picks up that sleek new pocket dictating machine and passes judgment on your future. That's a heavy-duty decision, yet I'm astonished at how few job candidates take their own futures seriously enough to record or organize their notes on the interviews that are going to have such an impact on their lives.

If the company that interviewed you is going to write a report on you, the impression you made, their evaluation of your professional and personal skills, shouldn't you, too? If you're going to put your future and your fate in anyone's hands, it should be your own. You have your *own* evaluation to make, impressions about your performance and about the company.

Those of you who have read either *Swim with the Sharks* or my second book, *Beware the Naked Man Who Offers You His Shirt,* should know by now what's coming next.

First, there was the Mackay 66 Customer Profile. Then, came the Mackay 33 for Managers. What else but the Mackay 22 Job Finder?

Simple discipline. Basic questions. But for my money, simple and basic are the only way to go.

Was I smart enough to use this form when I got my first job? No. But my first job was pushing a broom in a paper warehouse. You won't need this to get a job like that, but, on the other hand, a broom job may not be what you're after. It took a few years of nonbroom experience to dream this up.

Did I strongly suggest that my kids use it when they launched their first job hunts? Let's put it this way: Do you know how much it costs to field-test a new concept these days when you can't lean on your relatives? However, although I was ultimately successful in getting a couple of Mackays to use the Mackay 22, the experience taught me another painful lesson: There are three ways to get things done.

1) Do them yourself.

2) Hire someone else to do them.

3) Tell your children not to do them.

About this form: Obviously, you don't flip it out during your interview. Don't refer to it, either. The job interview is a corporate ritual, and your role in this mating dance is not to take control but to react intelligently and creatively to the signals you get from your interviewer. Getting the job is always going to be your number-one priority, but getting the answers to the questions about the job is right up there as a close second. Complete the form as soon as possible after your interview, while it's still fresh in your mind.

1. Date of interview_____

   Name of firm _____

   Address and phone no_____

   Interviewer_____

   Title_____

2. Describe position being filled _____

3. Last person in job left because _____

4. Position reports to_____

   Title_____

   Who reports to this position ? _____

5. Job's key duties_____

6. If last person in job succeeded, why?_____

   If last person in job failed, why? _____

7. Are there chances to get ahead? _____

   Describe _____

   Can you move laterally within the company to other departments requiring other skills? _____

   Describe _____

   Does the company encourage educational and training programs ? _____

   Describe _____

8. Would relocation be necessary now? _____

   In the future? _____

   Probable? _____

9. Describe the "ideal" candidate _____

10. What important information did you learn about pay, benefits, etc.? (Keep a light foot on the gas pedal here. You and your interviewer both know you're interested in this subject, and he or she will get to it if your're patient.)_____

11. When can you expect a decision? Was the interviewer specific? Vague? _____

12. What were the five most important questions asked you?

    (1) _____

(2) _____

(3) _____

(4) _____

(5) _____

13. What were the three most difficult or embarrassing questions?

(1) _____

(2) _____

(3) _____

14. What three things did the interviewer seem to like most about you or your background?

(1) _____

(2) _____

(3) _____

15. What reservations or concerns did the interviewer reveal?_____

What did you say or do during the interview that you wished you hadn't? _____

16. What important new information did you learn about this company that you might be able to use later? _____

_____

17. In what ways would this job/company be a good fit?

    _____

    In what ways would it be a poor fit? _____

18. Did you mention any references? Which ones? Have you alerted these people they may be called on to be a reference for you and do you feel they will give a positive response? _____

19. How did the interviewer describe your potential boss

    _____

20. Is this the kind of person you would trust? Feel comfortable working with? _____

21. Did the interviewer mention any special conditions under which you might be offered the job?_____

    Did you mention any conditions for you to accept it?

    _____

22. Fresh from the interview, what would be the biggest attraction to you in taking this job?_____

    The biggest drawback? _____

    Complete this form as soon as you can after your interview, because research tells us that we forget 70 percent of what we've heard within three hours. Then use it as a reference tool as you move along toward getting the job you've always wanted.

(Because I believe so strongly in preparing to win, I've also included a questionnaire you can use to get ready before you ever go to your first interview. You'll find "The Mackay Sweet Sixteen" in Appendix B.)

34

HOW I GOT THE JOB I WANTED, #4

It was 1974. Woodward and Bernstein had made journalism a profession of undergraduate dreams. It seemed like everyone wanted to become an "investigative reporter"—a redundancy, if there ever was one, since all reporters investigate.

I had been out of college for a few years and was working as a book editor but my true love was journalism. At the age of twenty-seven, with the undergraduate schools churning out wannabe Woodsteins at an incredible rate, I figured it was then or never. So I started applying to newspapers.

And applying and applying. The economy was in the doldrums and I was getting the standard "We have no openings at the present time but should things change, we'll keep your application on file." Unfortunately, I wanted things to change in my lifetime.

Obviously, I had to do something to make me stand out.

So I did.

I selected the five papers that, if I had a magic wand, I would go "poof" and find myself working at one of them. The *Los Angeles Times* was one. The *St. Louis Post-Dispatch*—I had never been to St. Louis at that point—was another. And, there was, of course, the *Washington Post*. In lieu of a magic wand, I took five twenty-dollar bills and cut each of them in jagged halves. I wrote to the editors of the five papers enclosing half of a bill. I told them that I realized they probably had no openings and were probably receiving hundreds of applications, but all I wanted was a little bit of their time. If they would only agree to have lunch with me, I would bring the other half of the twenty and pay. (It was 1974. You could still get a pretty decent lunch for twenty bucks.)

I got some very funny responses, but the one that *counted* came from Ben Bradlee, editor of the *Washington Post*. He said that ever since Watergate, even half of a twenty made him nervous. So he was passing it and my letter on to Dick Harwood, who had been national editor at the *Post* and recently named editor-in-chief of the *Trenton* (New Jersey) *Times,* a paper the *Post* had just bought. Harwood was intending to expand the staff at the *Times* and might be interested in my resume.

Harwood was interested, I was hired, and the lunch was pretty good, too.

Besides working as a book editor and a reporter at the *Trenton Times,* I have written seven books, ranging from the best-selling *Last Chance Diet* to a children's book, *Why Do I Have to Wear Glasses?*

Sandra Lee Stuart
Wynnewood, Pennsylvania

35

WHAT TO DO WHEN THEY FINALLY HAND YOU THE BALL

Countless job candidates come to an interview beautifully prepared to answer questions. The mistake they make is, they're not prepared to ask them.

At some point in every serious professional job interview, you're going to be asked if you have any questions of your own. This is not the time to ask about salary and benefits. Your tactics aren't to probe for information on your personal needs. This is the courtship phase, a long way from any permanent relationship. You have to strike sparks, differentiate yourself, show your people skills, be perceptive.

Do you know what kinds of job interviews your old,

cold interviewer really likes? Answer: Ones where he or she gets to recommend a candidate for the job. There are so many, many interviews where they don't. Successful candidates are the interviewer's hand-picked selections, and interviewers root for their choices the way handicappers root for their horses.

Interviewers serve as the gatekeepers not only of the company's personnel but of the company's values. They are there both to screen out candidates who don't fit and to be the first to tattoo "Company" on the foreheads of those who do.

Give them the chance to do the fun part of their jobs, reveal the corporate soul:

1. Ask about the company's values. Nothing is dearer to a company than its values. If you can ask a positive question that links the company's values to its performance, you've already gone a long way toward demonstrating that you're with the program. How about, "Last week I read in *Modern Envelope Reporter* that your quality program is knocking the industry's socks off, and your sales prove it. Isn't it pretty tough to maintain that standard of quality day after day?"

2. If the company is one of the industry leaders, have them tell you more. Successful companies, just like successful people, usually do not count modesty among their greatest virtues; nor are they immune to skillful flattery. Ask them how they got to be so good at what they do. "What does the competition see when they look at you?"

3. And then, there's the dark side of the moon, when the company's performance is the pits. Companies in trouble are like people in trouble: They want solutions. They're looking for role models, action plans, action people, to help transform them into winners again. They're hiring because they've got some ideas about what it will

take to put them back on their feet. They need the people who can help them execute those ideas, and provide some of their own. Ask, "Which companies in your industry do you feel you'd most like to resemble?" "How do you plan to achieve that?"

4. Listen to the answers. Don't make it appear that you're more interested in your own clever questions than you are in hearing and reacting to the responses.

5. Be perceptive, not contentious. Don't show off by asking for the interviewer to act as company spokesperson and explain some embarrassing gaffe like an environmental fine. You're not there to sit in moral judgment. If the company's behavior has offended you, this probably is not the place for you to seek employment. You're an interested and respectful listener, not Mike Wallace trying to bag another corporate pelt for his trophy wall.

6. Don't forget to read the walls and desks. You may be talking to the consummate company person, but he or she is still a human being with a three-year-old's finger painting framed and propped up on the desk, perhaps next to a team photo, and with a Rotarian award on the wall. You should somehow be able to relate to one of these, or you should consider applying for a job someplace where you don't have to deal much with people, like a fish farm. Didn't Uncle Charlie belong to Rotary? Doesn't your five-year-old love to finger paint? Well, by now, you know what to do.

36

MORE QUESTIONABLE PRACTICES

Let's turn up the burners a bit on our questioning game plan. I'm going to assume that your relationship with the prospective employer has passed through the blind date stage and you're now eyeing each other seriously as marriage partners. There's no more need for wow-aren't-you-wonderful questions. You are digging for the kind of real inside information that may help you decide whether or not you want to enter into a permanent arrangement. We'll also assume you've already done your homework by checking with your own sources, like friends who are employed with the company, vendors, public information available at the library and through investment firms, and you haven't come up with diddly.

What do you probe for and how do you do the probing? Something to keep in mind—every company has its
soft spots and family skeletons.

The flip side of a company that's dynamic and action-
oriented is that it's often an administrative nightmare flying
through space by the seat of its pants. Changes of policy
occur as often as changes of underwear, the organization
chart looks like a plate of linguini, and financial and operating reports could win Pulitzer Prizes for fiction. Another
common type, the highly structured company with deep
roots in the community, a long, proud history, ingrained
traditions, and a solid reputation for compassion and concern in caring for its employees, could be a bureaucratic
jungle, filled with dead ends and deadwood, baroque
office politics, featherbedding, blind alleys, meaningless
rules, and endless red tape.

In either case, your boss-to-be could be the perfect
stereotype of the company's personality: a driven, hyper,
ill-tempered, disorganized, mad genius who won't let anyone else do anything or, equally unterrific, a kindly, charm-
ing, totally incompetent sloth, obsessed with meaningless
detail, who dithers endlessly and gets nothing done. To
find out if these extreme examples are looming in your
future, you have to ask some tactful but nosy questions as
the interview process clanks along to its grand finale:

"You're obviously going to the outside to fill this
vacancy. Is this an exception? Do you generally fill your
openings with outside candidates?"

"Have you had any big staffing cutbacks recently? Do
you expect any?"

The next four questions are more gutsy. You have to
be fairly far along in the hiring process and have established a good rapport with your interviewer before you
can ask them, but remember, we're playing for keeps
here.

"Every company has its strengths and weaknesses. What are they for your firm? In particular, what are this firm's strengths and weaknesses in dealing with people?"

"I don't want to pry, but you've obviously been a success in this firm, and I want to understand better what goes into making people successful here. What have been your biggest satisfactions and disappointments since you've been with this company?"

"I imagine that you do a pretty good job of keeping good people. When people do leave, however, what's the most common reason?"

"Could you give me an idea of what my potential boss is like? Are there particular qualities he or she is looking for in a candidate?"

If this sounds like sifting through other people's garbage, well, it is. So be it. The questions you ask today can save both you and your potential employer a lot of grief someday in the future. Also, if the atmosphere is favorable, why not ask to visit with a few of the employees? Because of the interest you are showing, your interviewer will only have *more* respect for you.

Don't expect miracles. You have to be able to sense how far you can push without generating resentment and a fatal backfire. And some firms and managers are cunning enough to give very misleading answers—just like the neighbors who are so afraid you'll find out they drink that they don't leave their empties in the garbage but haul them out to the city dump in the middle of the night.

37

THE TRICKLE-DOWN THEORY
THAT ALWAYS WORKS

Does prosperity percolate up from the bottom or trickle down from the top? Economists and politicians have been flinging statistics at each other forever on this one without persuading their opposite numbers, and no end to the argument is in sight.

Whether or not prosperity trickles down, attitudes do. A boss who leaves work regularly at four o'clock shouldn't be surprised if there's no one around the office to answer the phone when he calls in for his messages at five.

Twenty years ago, when the football head coaching job opened up at the University of Minnesota, my buddy Paul Giel, the athletic director, got me involved in taking a serious run at Bud Wilkinson. At the time, Wilkinson had retired from the head coaching job at the University of Oklahoma and was doing sports color commentary on ABC-TV at a hundred thousand dollars a year. He had been a former All-American end at Minnesota and still was widely regarded as the best college coach in the business.

So Giel and I went to Oklahoma to see him. We had a four-hour meeting and laid a five hundred thousand-dollar package on the table, big, big money for those days. Wilkinson was impressed but noncommittal.

"There are a few things I'll have to check out before I can let you know," he said.

He called us back the next week.

"There's nothing the matter with the numbers," he said. "In fact, they're better than I would have asked for myself, so please don't think that by increasing them my answer will be any different. It won't. I've checked very thoroughly, and thought very carefully, and I have to turn you down. For one very simple reason: I can't win at Minnesota. There's no commitment at the top. I don't want to go anywhere where I can't develop a winning program." No argument we could dredge up would change his mind.

Because what he said was true.

For whatever reasons—historical, cultural, political— the real powers at the University of Minnesota were not committed to a winning football program. Minnesota's subsequent record was black-letter proof that Wilkinson was right. There was no place at Minnesota for a coach determined to create a winning football program. Now that's no tragedy. Harvard and the rest of the Ivy League aren't committed to winning football programs either, nor is Oxford, nor the Sorbonne, nor countless other excellent universities. But in those cases, there was no misreading the message that came direct from the top: We have other priorities.

In Minnesota's case, the message trickled down in a less straightforward fashion: We'd like to win if *you* can make it happen, but *we* won't make the commitment.

Corporate attitudes are deployed in the same fashion, by ripple effect. The Optimum Leader is the pebble. With every splash he or she makes, the waves ripple through the organization, washing over every person, every mission statement, every long-range plan, every hire. He or she is in charge. His or her vision and the corporate vision are one and the same.

A strong leader runs a tight ship and keeps a steady course. Every splash this type of boss makes can be felt at the farthest corner of the corporate chart.

A weak splasher skips across the water, generating weak ripples, leaving everyone to fend for themselves. Will the boss go for it? Who knows? There are no clear signals. Splish, Splash, Glub, Glub.

Giel and I learned to live without Bud Wilkinson as the University of Minnesota's football coach and to accept the less than committed mindset that defined the administration's attitude toward intercollegiate athletics.

It taught me a lesson.

Ambiguous commitment produces mediocre results.

In everything.

No matter how attractive the offer, before you go to work for a company with a less than winning record, be prepared to find that below average is the norm: in coworkers, in product quality, in personal satisfaction.

Bud Wilkinson didn't feel he could work in that kind of environment.

Can you?

38

EARLY BIRDS GET THE WORM.
LATE BIRDS GET THE JOB

From the time we were kids, we've been force-fed the idea that *first* is best. We seldom realize that it doesn't always work that way. Sometimes *last* is best.

The conventional wisdom is to be first across the finish line, first in our class in grades, first in line for chow, first for tickets to the Madonna concert, and first to be interviewed by a prospective employer. A, B, C, and D work just fine. E doesn't. You never want to be the first candidate to be interviewed.

Give any savvy advertising agency an opportunity to select a time slot for a client pitch and they'll always take the last one, the one closest to the moment when the choice of agencies is made. These people make their living understanding human nature. They know what makes people tick psychologically.

Clients tend to regard the first pitches they hear as preliminary fights on a boxing card, not to be taken terribly seriously. They're on the card to give them an opportunity to see what's out there, to try out their questions and sharpen their reactions in preparation for the main event.

The same kind of buildup is used in assembling a concert performance. You start with the aptly named "warmup" acts. They're the appetizers. The headliner is the main course.

If you want to see true creative ingenuity in action, you should see what happens when a prospective client tries to schedule an agency pitch.

"We wish we could take the Monday eight A.M. slot, but all our account people will be having open heart surgery that day. They should be up and around by Wednesday afternoon, though."

With most openings, the company's job specs are likely to be vague at first, becoming clearer only after they have had the opportunity to interview (and argue about) a couple of candidates. You don't want to be the test dummy, smashed into a wall, so the company can design a better vehicle for someone else.

If you are going for a job interview, try to learn how many candidates have already been seen. If you ask, and the recruiter dodges the question, consider yourself to be among the first or second entrants, and be prepared with a good, believable reason why a later time would be better.

If you can't avoid being first, try to leave the interviewer with something to think about: "I know you'll be talking with other candidates, and it's hard to remember the first person you talked to, but I'm committed to doing everything I can to work for your company, and I'd like to be asked back for a second interview."

Norman Vincent Peale tells the story about the eager job applicant who sees a help-wanted ad in the paper and rushes down to apply. By the time he arrives, there are at least two hundred people lined up waiting to be interviewed. After waiting in line for some time, he bolts out, runs to the front, where a woman is ushering them in one at a time, and says, "My name is Bruce Madison and you tell the people who are doing the hiring in there that I'm fifty-third in line and don't hire anyone until they've talked to me." He got the job, of course.

The Bible is right, the last shall be first, but you don't want to wait till you get to heaven to prove it.

39

HOW I GOT THE JOB I WANTED, #5

My story occurs in 1949. One of my graduate school professors told me about a job opening as advertising manager of a chain of ready-to-wear stores specializing in large size women's apparel. My professor doubted that they would even consider a twenty-two-year-old *girl* for such a responsible position. Previously, the slot was always filled by men. He suggested that there would be no harm, he supposed, in trying, especially since I was being granted my master's degree that week.

I decided to hand-deliver my presentation, which

consisted of a brightly colored binder (the kind used for term reports, book reviews, etc.). On the outside of the binder I glued a pair of ruby red dice (set to total eleven, of course!)

Below the dice I printed this query: *Willing to gamble, Mr. R? With these dice, how can you possibly lose?* Inside the binder, I pitched my gimmick. I stressed the fact that being female for this position was an *asset* rather than a liability since a female knew, instinctively, how to reach other women. I added that being twenty-two was also an asset—that I was young enough to be flexible, old enough to know the meaning of responsibility. I concluded with another query. *Mr. R., wouldn't you really want someone with a master's degree in* RETAILING ... just for the extra knowledge?

Under this, I pasted a copy of the award-winning suggestion I had had accepted by a leading retailing publication and for which a stipend of fifty dollars was given to me.

Two interviews later, I had the job and the *New York Times* saw fit to print my picture and a lengthy article because of my youth and sex.

I went on to spend the next twenty years in a variety of other interesting jobs. Some were part-time, some full-time. During all these years, many people said to me, "You were so lucky to get all these interesting jobs!" It was much more than *luck*. It was a well-planned campaign, using colorful stationery, brightly colored large envelopes, colored pens. Perhaps most important when answering blind box ads in the Sunday *New York Times* was going physically to the Times Building some time on Sunday or very early on Monday morning with my colored envelopes and handing them to the clerk for immediate distribution to the various box numbers. They were almost always the first letters received ... ahead of any that were mailed.

Laurel H. Grell
North Stratford, New Hampshire

P.S. 'Fess up. Didn't you open the oversized red envelope with so many stamps ahead of other mundane envelopes? It really works.

(It sure did, Laurel! You had no way of knowing when you answered my blind ad asking for unusual stories about job hunting that you were writing envelope testimonials to an envelope manufacturer. How could I ever turn down the chance to let the world hear from someone who attributes their success, in part, to the Power of the Envelope?)

40

DIALING FOR DOLLARS

The interview is over. The interviewer closes by saying, "We'll get back to you," as in, "Can't we just be friends?" or "I'm not ready to make a commitment. I think we should start seeing other people."

Don't let yourself get maneuvered into this hopeless dead end. Always try to position yourself to be the one to make the call.

"I'm afraid I don't have an answering machine."

"I'm out all day."

"I have a very sick relative in the hospital."

"I have a very sick relative at home."

Followed by:

"I'd like to call you back later in the week, if that would be all right."

Followed by:

"In that case, would next Monday or Tuesday be all right?"

Followed by:

"Well then, how about Wednesday or Thursday?"

Whatever. Who needs to have their nerves jangled every time the phone rings, waiting for the fickle finger of fate to land?

Try to control the agenda. The funny thing is, this strategy works most of the time. When you have the chance to lead, why choose to follow?

41

USING YOUR HEAD TO GET YOUR FOOT
IN THE DOOR

In *Sharks,* I wrote that the biggest single mistake a manager can make is a bad hire. And yet they're made all the time. If a human resources or personnel officer can claim a success ratio of 75 percent, they're bordering on the genius category because so much of the hirer's job is instinctive rather than scientific. Like real life.

A man and woman can date each other for years, but let them marry each other and they will know more about each other within weeks than they knew during their entire previous history together.

Or, let's say two married couples are the best of friends and have been neighbors for twenty years. One day one couple calls the other couple and says, "Hey, we've got a great idea. Why don't we go to Europe together for three weeks?" Result: When they get back there's a house on the block for sale. The two couples never speak to each other again.

An employer can interview a prospect for months, put him or her through every kind of boot camp drill, get to know his or her golf game so well the employer can tell within ten yards where the prospect's slice will land, exchange dinner invitations, check out the spouse's talents for the tango. Result: Two weeks after the hire, the employer is reaching for the Maalox and looking for a replacement.

There is no single question, no magic formula, to guard against failure in any enterprise involving human beings. We do the best we can.

The most common pitfall recruiters face is to be dazzled by personality. The 25 percent failure rate experienced even by ace recruiters is usually the result of confusing interview skills with job skills. We're all vulnerable to charmers.

The best way recruiters can protect themselves is to extend the process long enough to see candidates under as many varied conditions as possible. As we've seen, that doesn't always work. Here are a few more tricks of the trade candidates should know about:

1. Are your references what you claim they are? Are you concealing some bad ones? Recruiters check references more carefully than ever these days. The harder they dig, the more they find. Don't fake it, whether it's school, employment, or personal references. Often, when recruiters are not satisfied with the first set of references, they ask for more. If there are unexplained "gaps" in your job history, you should be able to cover them with some

kind of constructive effort, like school, volunteer work, individual entrepreneurship. Thankfully, parenthood is increasingly acceptable.

2. Do you meet the job specifications? Many job failures are the result of an imperfect match between the person and the position. A candidate eager for a job will say just about anything to demonstrate his or her qualifications. It's up to the recruiter to be focused, to have a clear understanding of *exactly* what skills are needed and not to be led off-course by a winning smile. Listen carefully to the job requirements. If you don't have the training or background described in the job prospectus, be up-front about it. Discuss whether you can still qualify for the position through on-the-job training or further education.

3. Do you know how to think? Note how the interviewer's questions are geared to open your thought processes for inspection, not just merely to elicit a mechanical response, like "I designed fifteen computer programs." What did the programs accomplish? To what extent did you involve users in the design process? How much did the programs help solve user problems? How many led to other, systems-wide streamlining in the company? Recruiters are looking for qualitative responses, not quantitative ones.

4. What are your work habits? Note how the interviewer wants to know where your ideas come from. Do you take all the credit yourself? How do you work as a team member? How will you fit in with the people you will be working with? Will they want to work with you or will they avoid you? When you answer a question, are you direct or evasive? Responsive or vague? Wordy or succinct? Here's where your interviewing skills are likely to match your job skills.

5. Are you truthful? Whether it's references, accomplishments, skills, whatever button is being pushed, the

interviewer is always looking for evidence of dishonesty, or, almost as bad, bragging and exaggeration. Don't even think about trying any of them. Getting caught here is a hit below the water line and fatal to your chances.

Think like a recruiter and you can sharkproof yourself for your next interview.

42

KURT EINSTEIN'S 20 MOST REVEALING INTERVIEW QUESTIONS

During the years I traveled the speakers' circuit, I never met anyone with a keener mind than Dr. Kurt Einstein. Following Kurt on the dais was the equivalent of trying to put over a fiddle act just after a Heifetz performance. He was a masterful teacher, and it was a privilege to be both his student and his friend. Kurt had extensive practical business experience and had trained thousands of executives and job seekers. Before he died, he let me use the questionnaire he developed for his seminars on personnel assessment. I suggest you practice answering these questions. If you can get to the point where you can handle them, I think you'll be able to carry off any interview successfully.

Kurt presented this material in his seminars titled "Picking and Keeping Winners." As you can see, the material is given from the perspective of the interviewer, not from the perspective of the interviewee. No matter. What that means is you're going to get a bonus—an insight into how the interviewer tries to set the stage psychologically for your session. So just turn your chair around when you go through this opening stuff and imagine how it looks from the other side of the table.

INTRODUCTION

It is not likely that you will feel comfortable with, or use, all of the questions which will be discussed. You should apply only those which fit your style or you will transfer your discomfort to the interviewee and retard the effectiveness of the interview.

To get something out of the interview, take a minute to recognize and observe a few basic facts before the presentation begins:

1. While the questions in themselves seem rather simple to understand, please be prepared to take notes. The reasons for asking them will demonstrate to you their complexity and also the benefits you will derive.

2. While interviewing, it is vitally important that you take your time. Rushing will lead to poor selection decisions and will also tend to put the candidate under inappropriate stress. Make certain that the candidate understands that you are interested in spending a great deal of time, do not want superficial answers, but would like replies in as much detail as he or she is able to provide.

3. To the degree that you create an interviewing atmosphere which is relaxed and friendly, you will find that candidates are willing to open up and give you the

"straight poop." In fact, it is strongly recommended that you not begin using these questions until this atmosphere has successfully been established.

4. Please note that close-ended questions which can be answered with "yes" or "no" are leading questions and should be avoided under all circumstances. Open-ended questions which cannot be answered "yes" or "no" produce valuable information which will help you to make a successful selection decision.

5. Sophisticated interviewing is both a science and an art form. All techniques which you will be learning today have been laboratory- and field-tested and will help you to gather relevant information. However, what you *do* with this information depends entirely on your judgment.

6. Interviewing is the ability to predict an individual's future performance and behavior. Consequently, an interview is complete only when the interviewer can determine, with a high degree of accuracy, what speaks for the candidate (areas of strength) and what speaks against the candidate (areas of weakness) and the reasons for both. Therefore, all discussions, inquiries and information gathering should be related to this one objective.

7. In the United States, EEO law does not allow any inquiry, whatsoever, unless the interviewer can explain why the inquiry is job-related. Otherwise, it is a violation of the law and must be avoided under all circumstances.

Questions

1. What have you been criticized for during the last four years?

_____

_____

2. Did you agree or disagree and why?

_____

_____

3. Where would you like to be in 3–5 years? 5–10 years?

_____

_____

3a. How do you expect to get there?

_____

_____

4. What would you like to change in this job to make it ideal?

_____

_____

4a. How would you describe the most or least ideal boss you could choose?

_____

_____

5. What activities in your position do you enjoy most?

_____

_____

6. How would you describe yourself in three adjectives?

_____

_____

6a. How would your subordinates or peers describe you with three adjectives?

_____

_____

7. Do you think you praise enough? If yes, ask: What makes you think so?

_____

_____

If no, why not?

_____

_____

8. What would you do if you detected a peer falsifying expense records?

_____

_____

9. What would you do if the company you had just joined gave you $3,000.00 to spend during the first year any way you felt appropriate?

_____

_____

10. If you had a choice, would you rather draw up plans or implement them?

_____

_____

11. State three situations in which you did not succeed. Why?

_____

_____

12. When you fire somebody, other than severing them from the company, what would be your key objective? Why?

_____

_____

13. What needs do you expect to satisfy by accepting this position?

_____

_____

14. What would you like to change in this job to make it ideal?

_____

_____

15. We all fib occasionally. Would you say something that is not entirely true? Give me three examples when you did.

_____

_____

16. What benefits can be expected from threatening an employee to do better? _____

_____

_____

16a. When would you do that?

_____

_____

17. If you encountered serious difficulties on this job, what would they be?

_____

_____

18. What are three things you are afraid to find in this job?

_____

_____

19. We all have negative areas we would like to improve. Do you agree? If you do, could you give me three areas in which you would like to improve?

_____

_____

20. How do you motivate people?

_____

_____

Now, do you want to see how your answers are perceived? Sure you do. First, though, read the questions again and write down your answers. Then go to Appendix A in the back of this book, and you'll find Dr. Einstein's observations … and mine.

43

WHAT INTERVIEWERS SAY BEHIND YOUR BACK

Every form of human activity seems to have its own insider jargon.

John Challenger, vice-president of Challenger, Gray & Christmas, of Chicago, a national outplacement firm, was quoted in the *Washington Post Service* as giving a few less than flattering descriptions of how job seekers are viewed from the other side of the desk.

Heaven Sent: an egocentric applicant who thinks
  everyone is waiting to hire him.
Don Quixote: the job hunter who holds out for the job
  he or she is unqualified for.

Rootbound: someone who refuses to move for a job.

Peacenix: laid-off defense worker.

Nester: applicant who hibernates in an office rather than pursue interviews.

Mailer: one who banks on resume mailings rather than face-to-face interviews.

Midnighter: person who waits until the last moment before severance pay runs out to start looking for a job.

Tree Hugger: someone who's worked for only one company for years.

Refusnik: anyone who doesn't bother to job hunt due to the mistaken belief that employers will call.

Let me add a few more I've heard over the years:

Elvis Spotter: someone who believes name-dropping will impress the interviewer.

Gapper: someone with large, unexplained gaps in a resume.

Recycled: a person who has made a huge, unsuccessful attempt to try to appear ten years younger, wearing something like an ill-fitting toupee. (Why is it when you're talking to someone wearing one of those things, it's impossible to keep your eyes off it?)

Human Applause Meter: someone who thinks they're flattering you by chuckling, laughing, or giggling at everything you say.

Dapper Dan: the suit is so new it gaps about three inches from the collar of the shirt to the collar of the suit when he sits down.

Boilerplate Special: a resume that's made the rounds of every company in town.

Trying Out Their Nose Job: they "casually" lean over

the interviewer's desk, trying to read upside down what it is the interviewer has written about them on their pad.

Bullwinkle: slips on the floor, falls out of the chair, trips on the rug, spills coffee on the desk, can't open or close the door. You'd be amazed at how many of these there are.

Nixonlip: sweaty upper lip and forehead. From the Nixon/Kennedy presidential candidate debates, the first to be televised. This is what many people think cost Nixon the 1960 election.

Strange Interlude: resume showing time spent in jail.

Faulty Research: phony entry in the resume, reference doesn't check out or gives a bad report.

Third-Degree Burn: degree listed in the resume doesn't exist.

Carpet Inspector: looked at his or her shoes throughout the interview.

Eyeball Inspector: told to make eye contact, this candidate's eyes *never* leave yours, drilling into your head with unblinking, robotlike precision.

Weak Report Card: bad resume or interview.

If you see yourself or any of your habits here, you better get rewired if you expect to get hired.

44

A FIRE IN THE BELLY

We've all walked by service establishments, like hotels and restaurants, and seen a sign in the window. "HELP WANTED. EXPERIENCE NECESSARY." The smart operators know that sometimes the opposite is true. By the time a chambermaid or a bellhop has logged a few years, too many of them are not only tired and surly, they're also unretrainable.

Before the dissolution of the communist state, no country could match the USSR for the dinginess of its restaurants and hotels and the incompetence of their service.

Switching jobs there required more paperwork than floating a junk bond issue here. Once a waitress, always a waitress. Tell Ninotchka that you'd found an "oh-no-ski!" in your borscht, and she'd thrust her clenched jaw at you, steel teeth and all, silently lip-synching Ivan the Terrible–type revenge … and stomp off to log a demerit in your KGB file.

A new hotel has recently been proposed by Western developers, and they want no part of the old Soviet tradition of service with a smirk. Their motto is, "HELP WANTED. INEXPERIENCE NECESSARY."

I was told recently about Todd Schrupp, a high school graduate in his early twenties, who is said to earn $75,000 a year as the track announcer at Calder Race Track in Florida. Obviously, Schrupp was far from being the only candidate for the job, yet despite only two years of experience in the racetrack industry, he got it. Why? They told him it was because of his freshness and enthusiasm. He hadn't been around the business long enough to become cynical about it.

When you interview for a job, don't overdo bragging about your experience and your past accomplishments. Interviewers get a little bored with hearing endless versions of the conquest of Mt. Everest. Over and over they've been told, "I've got fifteen years' experience," when what the candidate really means is they've had "one year's experience repeated fifteen times." What have you done to grow and to add to your skills over the years? What can you do for *them?* What new ideas, what needed skills, can you offer to meet *their* needs? Are you eager to infuse the company with energy and drive?

As Charles Kettering said, "We work day after day … to make the future better … because we will spend the rest of our lives there."

Why hasn't the company interviewing you hired from inside? Lack of experience?

No.

Lack of vision. If you can bring them the future, you have all the experience they need.

IV

HIRED!

45

DIANE'S STORY

Diane Dietz was a salesperson at Peavey Company in Minneapolis when the company was bought out by Con-Agra, another large agribusiness outfit, headquartered in Omaha.

"We were told no one would lose their jobs, but despite the promises, it happened. It was the first time I had been out of work and had to undergo a real job search. It taught me some things, mostly about myself.

"It taught me I had to be a risk taker (what I call 'pushing the envelope') if I wanted to find the job I really wanted. Typically, women are conditioned to be caretakers of others, not of themselves, even on the job. We had employees who were so into denial that they didn't start thinking of alternatives until their last day on the job.

"In my opinion, there are four essentials you need to find a new job.

"First, you have to research the opportunities. I know you say you should read the classifieds, but there are a lot of people who think, 'Nobody ever found a job in the newspapers.' Even for skeptics, though, the classifieds can be a big help if you learn to read them properly. Trends, for example. Classifieds will tell you the *kinds* of positions that are open. If one or two big food companies are advertising for salespeople, chances are there are openings at others who aren't advertising. What you do now is find out just who those others are. Usually, they're the smaller, more obscure companies. They also tend to be the more entrepreneurial and proactive companies. Talk to suppliers or vendors. In my case, I got names from food brokers, who supply almost all the companies in the industry. I actually got my first job from a classified, but not in the papers, in a trade journal, a very good place to look because often you'll find positions advertised here that won't be found anywhere else.

"Second, interviews. Preparation is the key, and your own mental preparation is just as important as knowing the right buzzwords about the company and the industry. We're all different. We're all unique. Know what qualities you have that can benefit an employer.

"In my case, I was looking for a sales position and I knew from previous experience that people who recruit salespeople tend to prefer generalists. But I had something else, too. As a former cereal chemist, I had a command of detail that is uncommon among salespeople. I tried to stress my ability to make a clear, logical presentation, while at the same time not frighten the interviewer into thinking I'd get bogged down in technobabble every time I made a sales pitch. Also, as a lab technician, I'd learned another skill that is desirable for salespeople—I had to be a quick thinker.

"Sometimes, while grain cars were sitting on the loading docks, I had to make a rapid analysis and an almost instant judgment whether or not the contents should be sent into production, sold, rejected, or renegotiated in price. Salespeople often face many of the same kinds of challenges.

"Big picture. Good eye for detail. Quick thinking. I went into every interview with a plan to get these points across about myself to indicate that I had ambition and ideas.

"The crux of it is this: I always felt I was interviewing the company as much as they were interviewing me. After all, it was my life and not just a paycheck that was at stake here. I never went in hat in hand. I could understand, appreciate, and be responsive to their concerns, but I had to maintain control of my agenda while they were pursuing theirs.

"Third, resumes. Stress accomplishments, not titles. And if there are those 'Oh, look at me' things you just have to get across, you're going to feel a lot less stress at interview time if you get them in the hard copy. So put them in your resume.

"Finally, most important is your own soul-searching. I think people have a tendency to start a job search by selling themselves short. They think, 'Boy, if I can only get a job as good as my last one.' I wanted to think in terms of improving on my situation, not just equaling it. I would hope and urge everyone out there who is able to, not to accept a job that is not what you want to do, but only what you can do.

"If you're ambitious to make people believe in you, you have to actualize that ambition. You can't just *say* you have ambition. You have to *show* it. You've accepted challenges. You've made things happen. You have a lot to be proud of. And you can make a contribution to the company you're interviewing."

I had lunch with this dynamic woman. She impressed me with her enthusiasm, dedication, and style, and I'm not surprised that she is now director of marketing for Malt O'Meal, a major agribusiness company headquartered in Minneapolis.

46

FOR JUST 90 PERCENT MORE
YOU CAN GO FIRST CLASS

The late comedian George Gobel used to have a tag
line, "For just a few pennies more, you can go first class."
If he were around now, he'd have to update his act.

The price spread between first class and coach may
have widened over the years, but one thing hasn't
changed—both parts of the plane still land at the same
time.

It remains a mystery to me why the airline industry has
never been able to make anything resembling first class
out of first class, and as for tourist, I won't bore you with
airline food, seat, and schedule jokes. This frequent flyer
has experienced them all.

It comes as a pleasant surprise to me that, as I am writing this, while flying Northwest #587 Orlando to Minneapolis, we may just have entered the new era of air travel.

The difference, as usual, is in the people, in this case the captain, Ken Watts.

He greets each of us as we come on board with a warm smile and the observation that it's a great day for flying and we can expect a smooth ride. A nice confidence-builder for the white-knuckle crowd. As far as the rest of us are concerned, it doesn't hurt to know that they haven't figured out a way yet to save a few more bucks by putting a chimpanzee at the controls.

No sooner are we airborne than the captain's smooth, professional announcer's voice comes over the loud-speaker. We get a guided tour of central Florida, including Disney World. Over half the passengers appear to be comprised of family groups, rather than the usual business crowd. They get a hoot out of the mile-high perspective on the place where they just spent their vacation.

Halfway home, and the captain says we have a little surprise for all the kids on board. The flight attendants will be coming through with platters of candy, subject, of course, to the consent of the parents. I pressed the call button and asked if I qualified as a kiddie. No question about it. Is all this Northwest's idea? Oh no, Captain Watts pays for it out of his own pocket.

And then as we're landing, "This is your captain speaking. For those kids who may be traveling for the first time, or anyone else who has an interest, please feel free on the way out to have your picture taken up here in the cockpit with me. And, incidentally, if you don't have a camera, no problem, use mine."

What's happening here? To begin with, I'm a bit of a naïf, so I'm going to believe that Northwest really does not program this or pay for the goodies. Yes, I do believe it even though Northwest gets every bit of the mileage out of it. Note also that the passenger load on this route has a heavy tourist component and tourists are discretionary travelers, with much more flexible schedules, and therefore a wider choice of airlines than business travelers. Northwest. Schmorthwest. What does it matter as long as we have a good time? Tourists actually *expect* that half the fun is getting there. Business travelers know better and, besides, they're a captive audience, like bus riders. Airline routes and schedules control their choice of carriers. Definitely not your soaring on the wings of eagles crowd.

So what we have here is a fortuitous matching of interests. Northwest has assigned a pilot for this route who meets the company's needs by meeting the needs of its customers. Presumably travelers will want to fly Northwest because Captain Watts is able to make them believe that three hours in a sardine can is like a ride at Disney World.

All Captain Watts gets out of it is to have his picture pasted into a few thousand family vacation albums.

Or is that all?

When you stop to analyze it, you realize that both employer and employee must realize what a valuable asset he is. He provides them with a competitive advantage on a route where the customers can be as picky as they care to be, and the only real difference between suppliers lies in the quality of the service, tiny intangibles like Captain Watts's personality.

Do you believe it doesn't really matter all that much? Well, maybe not, but the airlines believe it does, or why else would they be spending millions on campaigns like United's "Fly the friendly skies" and Delta's "We love to fly and it shows."

Think about it: Warmth of personality, common courtesy, and friendliness are the cutting edge of competition, the bottom-line difference between major American corporations. Which means this: When you can light up a room, you're always going to have happy landings professionally. Who says you can't put a price on a smile?

47

CREATE YOUR OWN BRAIN TRUST

A founder of one of the Twin Cities' largest law firms used to tell potential clients who were somewhat intimidated by the size and blue-chip reputation of his outfit that "we didn't get this way by overcharging people." Most of us fear hiring the best lawyer or best doctor or best financier in town not only because we think he or she will be too expensive but because we think "he or she wouldn't want to work for some small fry like me." Not so, in many cases. These top professionals didn't get where they are by gouging or by being snobs. They succeeded using the same formula that has always worked in this country: giving good value at fair prices and knocking themselves out to do it. Though their professions may be more intellectually demanding, they're no different from hungry fighters in any other business who clawed their way to the top. My experience is that they tend to be intrigued by a person—particularly a younger person without a lot of money or position—who has the brass to want to hire them. After all, they didn't reach the top by being wallpaper. Can you imagine yourself calling the fanciest hotshot lawyer or doctor or financier in town and saying you want to hire him or her?

"Why?"

"Well, you sell advice, don't you, and I'm told you give excellent advice."

"True enough, but what kind of advice do you want?"

"It's of a personal nature. You give advice of a personal nature, don't you?"

"Yes. But I specialize in dealing with corporate law/duodenal ulcers/financing of billion-dollar mergers and acquisitions."

"But, as you say, in the course of your practice you have to advise on matters with a lot of complicated personal factors involved, so you have to be just as expert on those things as well. And, of course, I'm willing to pay for your time. I'd like to hire you for one half-hour at your regular hourly rate for your advice. Your best advice. I can tell you that I'm one person who's a good listener and prepared to act on good advice."

If you can penetrate the golden mosquito netting you're bound to encounter and actually make that appointment, I'd sure like to be a fly on the wall during your meeting. I predict if you play your cards right you'll not only make a friend for life of one of the most influential and powerful people in town, you'll also end up with a lot more than a half-hour's worth of time and good advice.

You'd be surprised how many of the people who seem

so elevated above the cares of everyday life actually enjoy talking to real people instead of just the endless stream of fellow big shots who inhabit their lives. And how much they enjoy using their influence and seeing their advice acted upon. Most of us old geezers would like to be sought out by young people for our wisdom rather than just for the keys to the car.

When I was starting out, I leaned heavily on the accountant who helped me when I bought the bag of nuts and bolts that turned out to be Mackay Envelope. Until he passed away recently, I still leaned on him, often for advice on subjects far afield from his profession. The same has been true with my lawyer, my doctor, and even my old high school adviser. These wise men and women saved me from disaster more times than I care to remember.

That was then, this is now, so there's a new name you should add to your file of lifetime consultants that wasn't a necessity in my day but certainly is today: executive recruiter. Don't leave for work, ever, without one.

Over the years, I've become an adviser as well as an advisee. As an avocation, I've counseled hundreds of young people on their careers and have enjoyed enormous satisfaction because of their accomplishments. The side effects have also been a big plus. Along with the friendship of these kids has often come the gratitude and friendship of their friends and relatives.

Do I put them on my business prospecting list? No, but don't tell my sales manager, or he'll ask me for the names.

48

THE RED FILE

When I was a kid, one of my parents' favorite Sunday afternoon routines was the family drive. My sister and I would pile into the back seat, Mom and Dad occupied sacred territory in front, and for about two hours we'd cruise the neighborhood in our Pontiac. My parents amused themselves ogling the neighbors and comparing the state of their lawns to the National Standard, whatever that was, while I tried to get away with punching my sister without getting caught. If the outing was completed without serious bloodshed, we usually got an ice cream cone.

Families have since found better uses for their spare time, and generations of increasingly uppity kids have rebelled at the prospect of being locked up for an afternoon with their siblings, but part of the experience has carried over into my adulthood.

I still like to do a drive-around, though these days it's more of a risk. Anyone seen circling a block more than once is commonly thought to be trying to line up a burglary prospect. My motives are more prosaic. I've always found that if I want to buy a house I sure don't want to wait to see a "For Sale" sign on it. I pick out the houses that I want, which are the houses that knock me out with their curb appeal, knock on the door, and say to the owner, "I'm in love with your house. I have no idea if you ever want to sell, but if you do, I'm prepared to give you an offer immediately. And if not today, then next week, next month, next year." Sure enough, in the course of thirty years of astonishing homeowners with this brash proposition, I've bought two beautiful houses that way.

It's not as nutty as it seems. It's simply a real-life application of one of my favorite aphorisms, "Dig your well before you're thirsty." If you're raising a family and building a career, you're going to make a move, on the average, once every five years. Why do it in a panic? Why limit yourself to what's in the classifieds? Be prepared. Lay the groundwork. Build an inventory of homes you'd like to own.

That's also what I've done when I wanted to expand our business. For two solid years, I searched all over the country to find and acquire another company. During that time, I targeted twenty-five different companies, made contact with all of them to see if they wanted to sell (none did), but positioned myself to win in the long run. I had established the odds in my favor at 1 to 25. Eventually, something was going to happen. Someone was going to die unexpectedly, someone was going to want to sell his or her business and retire, someone else was going to find his or her kids didn't want to be the envelope kings of

Sioux City, and, eventually, something did happen. Months after we had spoken with a competing envelope company, and gotten no response, the owners eventually contacted us, and we are still in negotiations.

Even if you have a job, you can use that same strategy. Do you have a dream company? A dream position? Knock on the door. Let them know. "My dream is to work here no matter what the odds are today, and I'll keep coming back for years until I get a crack at it. Just allow me the courtesy of keeping in touch with you."

Build on that concept by keeping a "Red File." Mark it "Insurance Policy." Include your dream job, but also load it with every potential job you may want to look at in the future, no matter how far out that job may sound to you today. Stay abreast of parallel jobs in your industry and in related fields that may open up in the future.

Your job is to be patient, position yourself well, and look for opportunities.

Thousands of years ago a mighty king ruling over his kingdom sent the word out that he was looking for someone who could teach his horse to fly. On a routine day while the king was holding court, his guards threw before him a beggar caught stealing some jewels. "Take the man away and behead him."

"But, my king, my king, I can teach your horse to fly. Just give me two years and I know I can do it." The astonished king said, "You can?" "Yes, yes, I know I can." "Granted. Spare his life. Take him away."

As the guards were dragging him away, one guard said, "You fool, what did you promise that for?" "Look," said the beggar, "in two years, I may be dead. The king may be dead. Or who knows, maybe I can teach the SOB to fly."

Keep your options open, establish the odds in your favor, and one day you'll get your chance.

49

WHERE THE BUGGY-WHIP MANUFACTURER DESCRIBES THE WORLD OF THE FUTURE

I'm not the one to tell you where the technology curve is going to be ten or twenty years from now. I can tell you this: Don't be too quick to believe anyone who says they know. When I got out of high school in 1950, ballpoint pens were still something of a novelty. And they leaked. An outfit called the Monroe Calculating Machine Company had just introduced a new product they claimed would someday be as widely used as a typewriter. They called it a calculator. Television, jet travel, automatic transmissions on cars, air conditioning, all were in their infancy. They revolutionized society in ways we could never have imagined. Television is the obvious example. But take a somewhat less obvious one, air conditioning, and its spinoff, better refrigeration systems. These developments weren't just a means for achieving creature comfort.

Because of our ability to push freon around a copper tube while we blow a fan over it, we've experienced a total revolution in eating habits, from fast foods to gourmet cooking, accompanied by a massive upheaval in the food industry. Now we can flash freeze freshly processed food and ship it rapidly to far-flung markets. Enter the Big Mac. Ain't progress grand!

And consider the social changes air conditioning has brought. They're even more dramatic than the industrial ones. Air conditioning helped bring about the rebirth and resurgence of the South. The old Confederacy was in an economic depression from the Civil War until after World War II. Air conditioning opened it up to northern investment capital, real estate speculation and development, and created a whole new business climate.

I don't want to give air conditioning more credit than Martin Luther King, but you get the idea. Technological change propels social change in ways we can't imagine.

The point is, you don't have to be a scientific genius to prosper from a scientific breakthrough.

When you're riding a technological wave, there are no limits, none, on how far and where it can take you, but one thing is certain: It is change in social trends, not the increase in productivity, that will have the biggest impact.

There are a couple of trends that even a guy who still writes most of his stuff with a number 2 pencil can figure out. The world of the twenty-first century will be a world in which we will no longer be able to afford to be so totally dependent upon fossil fuels for energy. They're depleting, they're polluting, and because they're largely under the direct control of unstable, foreign governments, they're unreliable. In the seventies, we figured shale oil was going to solve all that. It didn't, but the basic problem hasn't gone away either, so be prepared for a world where commuting and inner-city domestic travel will no longer be dominated by one-person occupants in six-person automobiles.

We've only begun to see the effects of the transmission of information over telephone lines. One effect is going to be its heavy-duty impact on the newspaper business. Today, if you have a computer, a modem, a printer, and a subscription to one of the popular interactive personal services like Prodigy, you not only can get the national news instantly, with a semiprimitive video accompaniment, but you can, if you're a print freak like me, make a permanent hard-copy printout of whatever it is you want to save. We're only a nanosecond away from adding newspaper-quality photography, the comics, the classifieds, the local news, and all the rest of the components we need to duplicate our daily papers.

Another telephone application, the fax machine, will not be a great help to your friendly envelope manufacturer. Why is it I can visualize a world without oil, but not a world without envelopes?

Our nation is beginning to turn inward. We have the wealth, the energy, the resources, and now, hopefully, the will to meet our great domestic needs. The physical infrastructure of our cities and counties and towns, neglected for decades, will be rebuilt. Bridges, schools, roads, parks, housing, all need massive amounts of work. It's a great place to refocus all the energy and resources we've spent on military hardware.

You're going to have to make a living in a world subject to all these changes. How do you play it?

I don't expect any rocket scientists to be reading this. They already have their work program laid out. It's the rest of us I want to assure that it's still possible to make a good living in an increasingly technological world.

One constant never changes. For the hard-working, reasonably intelligent generalist, the opportunities are as great as they've ever been: There can never be enough good people to sell, feed, clothe, house, educate, inform, distribute, entertain, preach to, and provide basic services to those who are going to be directly involved in the new technologies.

The other news is, don't worry too much if you are less than one of the great scientific minds of your generation. In every gold camp I ever read about, it's the saloon keepers who ended up with the dust and the miners who ate it.

50

SHRINKING YOUR WAY INTO A JOB

I'll call her Jorah Kipling, a cosmetics marketing executive in New York City. She lost her job of twelve years when her company was acquired in a leveraged buyout and the new ownership decided to "rightsize" to help pay off the enormous debt load.

Jorah had kept visible throughout the years by serving on numerous trade association groups and carefully grooming her public image through a few well-timed trade press interviews given to carefully cultivated media friends. When the evitable became the inevitable, she wasn't knocked off her pins.

Expecting that her job search might be a long one, Jorah had some stationery and business cards printed up

---

and called some of her industry contacts, offering her services as a consultant. The firms were reluctant to add permanent staff, but they were impressed with her credentials, so she quickly built a business with eight steady customers.

From the very start, Jorah had no desire to stay a consultant. But, she reasoned that she could use the consultancy relationship as a springboard: 1) to learn about job opportunities in the industry; 2) to showcase and position herself to potential employers.

Her business plan was shrewdly designed *not* to conquer the known world as a consultant but to serve as the vehicle for a "self-liquidating search plan" for a full-time executive job in her industry. Her plan had six elements:

1. *The foundation for the plan was in place before she was laid off.* During the time she was employed, Jorah kept up her contacts *outside* the company, burning no bridges, keeping visible in the industry, developing a reputation as an expert in her field.

2. *Establishing her consultancy, she focused on assignments that reinforced the image she had established.* She turned down several projects where she would have had to be a bit player or where the company wanting her services was a cut below her previous employer. She accepted only those assignments that gave her the opportunity to demonstrate the full range of her talents and only for companies she would have been willing to work for full-time.

3. *She kept score.* Jorah kept notes on every company she worked for, assigning them grades from A+ down to F for their performance in areas that would be important to her if she were employed there. What was their reputation in the industry? Did they treat their vendors fairly and pay promptly? (The best way to tell how they treated their

own employees.) Did they operate efficiently? Did they know how to make effective use of market research? Did they respond promptly to changing conditions? Were they stable financially? Did they deliver on their promises?

4. *She kept her ears open.* Jorah learned as much as she could about each of her client's business plans. Being a consultant is an ideal way to study a company's stability and growth prospects. There are generally two kinds of companies: holding operations, milking existing products for as much profit as possible by cutting expenses to the max and pushing up prices until consumers stop buying; or growth operations, constantly on the prowl for new products, expanding lines, broadening markets.

5. *She made the conscious decision to cut back her business rather than expand it.* After six months, Jorah's client list was down to five. After nine months, just three. Instead of adding more clients, Jorah used the information she had gained to weed out clients who were nonstarters as potential employers. She concentrated on the three remaining who met her criteria.

6. *She acted like an employee rather than a consultant.* Did you ever meet a consultant who didn't turn on the meter every chance he or she got? Not Jorah. She didn't charge for the courtesy projects, like a letter to a supplier or massaging a little ad copy, that other consultants used for piling on big time. She sent a bill, of course, indicating the work done, but instead of a big number in the right-hand column, there was an "N.C." for "No Charge." And she made it a point to drop her clients interesting items from the trade press.

Did Jorah finally get a job offer from one of her favored clients? No. Within a year she got *two* job offers, and accepted a full-time position as the market research director of a cosmetics company twice the size of her previous employer. The only thing I questioned was: Given what happened to her the last time she took a job, why that particular goal in the first place?

"I know there's no real security in this business," she told me. "But I wanted the backup and the prestige of a major job at a major company. Besides, I can do it all over again if I have to."

Given her track record, I believe her.

51

THERE'S NO BUSINESS THAT ISN'T LIKE SHOW BUSINESS

When was the last time you saw a classified ad for actors? If you employ actors, you don't have to advertise. They'll find you. For those in the profession, it's a lifetime of hiring agents, making the rounds, auditioning, and rejection, rejection, rejection. Even those who are currently working are rarely able to look beyond the next paycheck. When one gig ends, they can never be sure of the next. They face a neverending series of hearing you're-not-quite-right-for-the-part rebuffs and finding careers truncated by changing looks and changing tastes. Yet actors accept chronic unemployment as one of the vagaries of their profession and not as a personal commentary on their value as human beings.

Even though our rapidly changing economy seems to be reaching the point where many of us seem to enjoy no better job security than actors, our mindsets are a long way from accepting the same kind of professional instability they do.

Yet there are certain actors' habits any of us would do well to imitate.

In 1992 during Super Bowl week, which was held in my back yard at the Minneapolis Metrodome, Larry King and I were taking in an NFL extravaganza the Saturday night before the game. Tony Bennett was entertaining on stage. In the middle of Bennett's act, King leaned over to me and said, "This guy has sung some of the same songs for thirty years and he still makes every performance seem like he's more thrilled and excited about it all than anyone in the audience."

That's a pro. He gives it everything he's got, every time, just as if it were his first and last performance.

You may have to make ten, twenty, even a hundred pit stops to land one job. And you're going to start feeling awfully sorry for yourself, and if you're not careful, it's going to show. You have to dig down deep and somehow, some way, be as fresh, as happy to be there, as excited and as enthusiastic, as this sixty-five-year-old crooner, who's sung the same song five thousand times in five thousand smokey joints.

If he can do it, you can do it.

Here's how:

1. *Stay in character.* An actor playing Cyrano de Bergerac for the umpteenth time keeps his performance fresh by trying to project his character into new situations. What would Cyrano think about nuclear disarmament, microwave popcorn, nose jobs? Keeping the character alive offstage helps keep the character alive onstage.

Okay, now let's try that in the real world: You're an out-of-work engineer and want to be a working engineer again. Well, start working. Keep yourself sharp and fresh by looking at the everyday world, twenty-four hours a day, the way you would as a working engineer assigned to redesign the world around you.

2. *Change the line reading*. When Richard Burton played Hamlet on Broadway, they say he never read the same line the same way two nights in a row. Disconcerting for his fellow actors, but exciting for the audience. If there's more than one way to play Shakespeare or to sing Verdi, there's got to be more than one way to describe your career.

3. *Watch other performers in the same role*. One of the most common classroom acting exercises is for students to take turns performing a role or expressing an emotion in front of their class, then critiquing each other's performance. Just as in the videotaping exercise, watching other people do it opens you up to new interpretations and ideas.

4. *Break the mold*. Show business careers are based on the ability to cut through the clutter of lookalike performances and bring something new and exciting to a role. There are a thousand Elvis impersonators, but Elvis was the first and only Elvis. If the interviewer's question suggests a creative new idea to you, take a risk, express it. After all, the Japanese would not have kabuki theater today if a female Shinto temple attendant hadn't thrown a few songs and dances into the old, dull format that existed previously.

5. *Make believe it's your farewell performance*. When I played golf for the University of Minnesota, each spring we took a long road trip, one golf course blurring into another as we bounced through the Midwest. Midway through the Great Tour of 1952, I was certain my optic

nerves had locked and could only register the color green. My game began to show signs I had decided to withdraw by taking up residence in the rough. Then our coach, Les Bolstad, gave me the best advice I've ever received. He said, "Harvey, every single shot you take from now on, I want you to say to yourself, 'This is the last shot I'll hit as long as I live. Every drive is the last drive I will ever hit. Every sand shot is the last sand shot. Every putt is the last putt.'" When you put that kind of spin on your performance, your concentration will intensify, and you'll be amazed at how successful you'll be.

Entertainers use this same mental trick the instant they sense they're getting stale. "If I don't treat every performance as if it will be my farewell appearance, there's a good chance it may be," says Eddie Albert.

52

HOW I GOT THE JOB I WANTED, #6

I am a twenty-seven-year-old professional magician who moved from Milwaukee, Wisconsin to New York City in 1988 to pursue my career full-time. As a magician, I had two goals: to entertain for the president at the White House; and to be the resident magician aboard a cruise ship sailing throughout the world.

As a direct result of the following stunt, I realized both of these goals.

To gain the necessary recognition, I decided to become one of the hundreds of street performers entertaining on any given day in NYC. My plan, however, was to do this in such a way that I could not be ignored.

I created an image of a very wealthy "Wall Street executive" who, as a hobby, did magic. For five months, every day, I traveled around to different pre-arranged locations in Manhattan from noon until three. Arriving in a limousine, I proceeded to entertain the often vast crowds of people on their lunch hour.

At the conclusion of the performance, I produced, from my tophat a pile of real paper money, and I began to hand it out to the people I had just entertained, along with business cards which read: "Robin Hood, The Magician."

In interviews, I stated that I was a wealthy stockbroker from Wall Street who wanted to give something back to the community and was using magic as my vehicle. I wanted to entertain, I told the reporters, but in the process I wanted to thank the thousands of New Yorkers who support, by their tips, struggling, and often starving, street performers. This was my opportunity to reverse the situation and for the first time in history TIP THEM.

As you can imagine, word-of-mouth spread this story all over the Northeast and eventually led to my five-month stint with Royal Caribbean Cruise Lines and to my much anticipated gig at the White House. My contacts at both of these organizations had heard of "Robin Hood, The Magician," who was giving away money on the streets of New York.

Thomas Soloman
Jersey City, New Jersey

53

IS THERE SUCH A THING AS A GOOD JOB WITH A SHOVEL?

It's the classic Dumpie Dilemma: Should you move down the ladder to ensure your short-term survival, knowing that the long-term effect on your career could be damaging? I used to say "no," believing that every bad job you take weakens your resume and lessens your chance of ever being hired for a truly superior position.

But while that advice may have been valid during the much milder 1981–82 recession, this last recession has changed my mind. For one thing, despite appearances, it isn't over yet. Pick up any paper, and side by side with glowing reports about the jump in housing starts or increases in retail sales, there are articles like the one I saw recently in the *Albany* (New York) *Times Union* titled "2,500 line up for Niagara Mohawk jobs that don't exist."

Here's what two of the people standing in line had to say:

Sandra McKinley, thirty-one: "By trade, I'm a secretary, but now I'm willing to do anything."

Lorraine Fuchs, twenty-eight, who's an eyelash away from an accounting degree: "When I saw all these people I thought everyone was picketing. I've got a daughter to support, so I need a job."

There's no way people in this situation can wait for the perfect job to come along. They're desperate, so desperate that they're applying for jobs where there aren't any.

When that happens in the kind of numbers it's been happening in all across the country, the rules get changed big time. Just as our old attitudes about retirement at sixty-five and "women's work" and "no minorities need apply" don't cut it anymore, so it is that employers no longer regard a ratchetlike upgrade with every job change as an essential feature of your resume.

Too many good people, through no fault of their own, have spent too long downsized or out of work entirely. No such thing as a good job with a shovel? Any job is a good job these days, and as more and more people are forced to take work wherever, any onus attached to accepting a lesser position has disappeared. For all too many people, the question is no longer whether to take the job but where to find one to begin with.

What can be done?

There's the Chinese solution. I remember landing at the Shanghai airport for the first time and seeing a thousand people with scythes and pitchforks alongside the runways doing what one guy with a Toro can handle over here. There's the Russian solution. Same kind of division of labor as in China, except everybody had a fancy title of some kind, usually very scientific-sounding, like "engineer in charge of landscaping on northwest quadrant adjacent to southeast runway at Moscow airport."

I'm not so sure the laissez-faire American solution to the problem is currently working any better than theirs did.

While I can help you to find a job, creating the job itself is an assignment of a much greater magnitude. As I look around, I share the despair and anger I see on people's faces as they search for jobs in a country where there is so much real work that needs to be done. As a result of our failure to provide these jobs, the gulf between the nation's haves and have-nots continues to widen.

For the second time in the last thirty years, South Central Los Angeles has been the canary in the coal mine, an early warning system signaling the growing danger to the entire nation that comes from neglecting the needs of those at the bottom of the economic ladder.

This used to be one area where the government understood that it had a responsibility as the employer of last resort. Lately, government has refused to play that role in any meaningful way. Although it is not government, but small business, that has always been our greatest source of jobs, government policy has to become more progressive. It has to give small business the incentive to rebuild and rehire and provide a safety net to fill any gaps in employment that remain.

Am I touching on politics here? You bet I am. Last year, after Peter Ueberroth was appointed to head the commission to put LA back on its feet, I gave a speech in Los Angeles in which I said, "I'm going to go out on a limb and predict that Peter is going to rewrite the history books in Los Angeles. He's going to put together a program second to none, and you won't believe the organization, and the clout, and the *results* of what one person can spearhead."

Like everyone else, I'm right some of the time, wrong some of the time, but for the first time and the only time in my life, Ueberroth was making a prophet out of me while I was still at the podium turning over my three-by-five cards and talking about "someday." This guy really is as amazing as I said he was.

One of the many casualties of the riots was a FEDCO store. When last seen, it was bobbing around in four feet of water, the interior and the structure itself totally destroyed. The "experts" told Ueberroth it would take nine months to twelve months to make it operative again. FEDCO executives called a summit meeting with the union employees, 80 percent of whom were minorities. They met with the suppliers. The message was the same to everyone: "There are 1,300 jobs at stake here. They say we can't do it. We don't have the skills. We don't have the energy. We don't have the will. We don't have the guts. We don't care. We aren't good enough. Well, are they right?"

Not hardly.

The indomitable human spirit, the power of commitment, teamwork, crisis management, focus, and the determination to show the "experts" what people can do when they care about their community and one another, rebuilt that store. In just *eighteen days*.

Eighteen days.

Good enough? No. A lot better.

When it was ready to reopen, 2,000 customers were ready and waiting to bear witness to the miracle. The grand opening ceremonies featured a forty-five-person, self-organized employee choir, but before it was over, the audience joined in and swelled their numbers to 450, and by the time the doors swung open, there wasn't a dry eye in the house.

And if you think this was one in a row, you're wrong.

Taco Bell was also leveled and burned to the ground. This time, sixty jobs were at immediate risk. But that was only the tip of the iceberg. The underlying stakes were far bigger.

Taco Bell management corralled a willing PepsiCo management, the parent company of Taco Bell, and beat the rebuilding record. Within 48 hours, there was a new restaurant, with grass growing around the edges, flowers blooming in window boxes, and another opening day ceremony that lifted spirits and renewed the sense of being part of something special for everyone who attended.

And what's on the drawing board next? Ten more Taco Bells in South Central Los Angeles.

It's not something you read much about in the papers. Riots are news. Opening a store or a fast food restaurant is what journalists call a "mego," as in, "my eyes glaze over." Just as whenever there's a successful cancer drive or an American Heart Association campaign, you may read about it, but it's on page 18E of the third section of the paper, buried next to the goiter ads. Our society craves sensationalism, we're fixated on the fires that burn, not the fires that warm, the fires that glow.

So little attention is paid, so few of us are aware, but what's being done right now in Los Angeles matters so much, we have to get the word out. There's work to be done in America. And plenty of it.

As capable as he is, Peter Ueberroth can't do it all.

And, he can't do it alone.

While I know there's no one who could equal the energy, determination, and imagination Peter brings to his assignment, I also know that it's going to take more than good will to heal the wounds, both economic and emotional, that have been opened in this recession.

It will take real money, a real commitment by government, the community, the private sector, and some fundamental changes in all of our attitudes.

We're past the point where we need to worry about sprucing up our resumes. We need to spruce up our concern for each other.

54

BASS ARE STILL WHERE YOU FIND 'EM

Fishfinder #1. Unless you do something pretty special, like mowing lawns for the only guy in town with a lawn mower, there is more than one person who could be your boss.

As we get more and more specialized in our skills, there are fewer and fewer people doing what we do and fewer people still telling us how they want it done. If you're a planning analyst at an engineering firm, it behooves you to know the planning director for at least three other firms in town. If you're a delivery truck driver for the corner dry cleaner, behoove yourself to meet three other dry cleaning owners who do home delivery in your neighborhood.

Why? Because today's competitor can always become tomorrow's employer. If you drive a dry cleaning truck, you've got something current nonbosses, who are those potential new bosses, want very, very much: customers so loyal to you personally many of them can't even remember the name of the dry cleaner you're working for now. So far as your customers are concerned, it's your services they're employing no matter whose name is on the truck. And don't think of it as disloyal. Who's going to cry for you in the front office if you're "downsized" out of a job?

Just remember, be discreet. Before you talk to any potential new employer, be sure there's no connection to your present outfit.

Years ago, in the early days of black and white television, the most popular show in Minneapolis was called "Masterpiece Theater." It was strictly local, ran on Sunday nights, and featured nothing but old movies. The sponsor was a local dry cleaning establishment called G&K Cleaners and the "host" was the owner, a fellow named I.D. Fink. In those days, there were no restrictions on the length of commercials, and those for G&K Cleaners were interminable. Every ten minutes or so, the movie would be interrupted with what seemed like a commercial of equal length consisting of Fink explaining some arcane feature of the dry cleaner's art in intricate detail. Fink was considered an extraordinarily dry speaker to begin with, and the subject was, if possible, even more so. I mean, who cares what they do when they dry clean your pants? The kicker was, unbelievably, these commercials worked. People loved them. And business poured in. In fact, G&K got so big that in order to disguise their almost total monopoly on the Twin Cities' dry cleaning industry, they ran some of their operations under different names. One day, folklore has it, Fink gets a call from an irate customer. He's watched "Masterpiece Theater" for years, believed every word Fink told him, and what happens, his shirt comes back with a spot still on it. He's had it. He's getting a new dry cleaner. Nothing Fink says helps. The customer slams down the phone. The next week the ex-customer's new dry cleaner appears at the door. It's the same driver as before. Only this time, there's a different name on the truck. It was that special rare case. Fink owned the only lawn mower in town.

There are two things to remember about the Fink Gambit: Be sure when you cast your line not to hook yourself in the seat of the pants. There are companies that operate the same businesses under different names. Be careful you don't apply to one while you're employed at another. It suggests a level of dissatisfaction with your current job that could be hazardous.

The other thing to store in your tackle box is not to give up just because you've gotten turned down by one branch of a huge chain. Even though these chains try to use uniform hiring standards, individual managers are still individuals. Many a candidate will apply to one store, one service station, or one dry cleaner in a national franchise operation and assume that a turndown means that the entire chain won't hire them. Well, that's not necessarily true. Supply and demand vary from branch to branch and from area to area and so do the attitudes and quirks of the person doing the hiring at each particular location.

The identical principle works in management. If you're a financial analyst, even if you're skunked at the regional headquarters in Kentucky, they could be biting at the same firm's headquarters in Illinois.

Fishfinder #2. You have a job? Lucky you. Work hard for yourself. Work hard for your family. Work hard for your future. But don't forget to work very, very hard for your out-of-work friends. Send leads to those in need. Call them every two or three weeks to bolster their spirits. Lest we forget, the iron law of human relations, "Be nice to the people you meet on the way up, because you might meet them again on the way down," has not been repealed. The friends likely to remember you if the pink slip lands in your lap are the ones *you* remembered when they were in the ditch.

55

YOU CAN BE AT YOUR BEST WHEN THINGS ARE AT THEIR WORST

Out of work or miserable in your job and feeling sorry for yourself?

Do you think the deck is stacked against you, that if only you were younger, or older, or better educated, or had better connections, you could get the right job?

You're not the first one to feel that way, but as tough as you may think you've got it, there are others who have beaten longer odds to become successful.

Mike Brewer spent the earlier part of the 1980s in Kauai, Hawaii, as a latter-day hippie. He passed his time body-surfing, running along the beach, and racing his ten-speed between Hanalai and Haena, the whole Iron Man bit, meanwhile trying to stay afloat by selling postcards made from his photographs of the local nature scene. Not too bad a life … better if you have a nest egg or your hero is Tarzan. But when you're broke and ambitious, living in a hut in the jungle on a diet consisting of bananas, mangoes, and papayas has its drawbacks, even in Paradise. And when the local marijuana growers make it clear that your presence as a photographer in their hemp fields could be life-threatening—to you—it's time to make a career move.

Brewer was no mere amateur photographer. He was an experienced and meticulous pro, so fussy about his work that the 110mm film he used couldn't be processed to his specifications on the islands and had to be sent to New York. His master plan was to create a portfolio of posters and advertising-quality photography of the exotic Hawaiian landscape and wildlife that would find its way into stock use, where it would be rented by advertising agencies and publishers. But he wasn't satisfied with his progress by the time he was driven from his Garden of Eden.

What made it tougher was that he had what amounted to only one arm.

A polio-withered arm may not be much of a professional drawback if you're sitting in an office all day, but photography, as practiced by Brewer, required nearly as much in the way of physical talent as it did creative. To shoot what he needed, he had to drag sixty pounds of equipment into, down to, up to, above, below, and through lots of places people with two arms didn't have the nerve or the energy to attempt.

To make it tougher, Brewer knew that to become a successful free lance, he not only had to overcome whatever physical barriers a person with no disability would face, he had to do more, endure more hardships, take greater risks, to create a body of work that would stand out from what the average, so-called normal photographer would produce.

After leaving his Garden of Eden, Brewer moved to the other side of the island, where he housesat, still trying to put together a portfolio. To get by, he photographed the showpiece homes dotting the Kauai hillside for the local real estate industry. Never one to do it by the book, Brewer took his pictures with his one good arm while hanging out of a helicopter, legs wrapped around a pole in the open doorway, to keep from falling out. Over a period of time, he put together a rather complete inventory of the island's real estate.

And then along came Hurricane Eva.

When it was over, everything was blown to hell for miles. There was over two hundred million dollars in damage.

Brewer immediately went back up in a helicopter and took more photographs, photographs of all the destruction Eva had done.

Now he had photos of what it had looked like before Eva hit, and what it looked like afterward, immediately afterward, before the Hawaiian National Guard moved in. Because once the soldiers had cleared away the rubble, most of the evidence of where the high-water mark had been would be obliterated. The high-water mark was the boundary for the insurance companies' pay-or-no-pay decisions, the essential dividing line between what is covered by hurricane insurance (above the mark) and what isn't. Brewer had to act before the bulldozers moved in, and he did. "I went down to the radio station in town and told them what I had done," said Brewer, "and they put it out, and within twenty-four hours, there they were, looking for me, the guys in suits in a place where nobody ever wore a suit. The Rolex watch team. The insurance agents.

"I was the only guy in the world who had exactly what

they had to have. The houses before. The houses after. The high-water mark. Everything. With my photographs they could establish or disprove liability."

Brewer sold those pictures. He went back up in the helicopter and kept taking pictures for six weeks. He made more money in those few weeks than he had made in any full year in his entire life.

Sure, Hurricane Eva was a disaster, a disaster for everyone but one person, the person who made his own luck. The photos Brewer took before the hurricane were valuable in themselves, but it was the pictures he took after the hurricane, the pictures any professional photographer could have taken, that made the Rolex boys come running. More importantly, the one-armed photographer had proved what no gilt-edged resume, no impeccable educational credentials, no job title, no steady progression up the corporate ladder could match. He proved that one arm can be better than two when it is attached to someone with the initiative and ability to seize the moment and make the most of what he had.

Mike Brewer left the islands with his nest egg and wound up back on the mainland. Today, he is a successful independent television producer.

"I still think I took some nature photos as good as anyone has ever taken in Hawaii. But, I'll settle for what nature gave me at her worst, and someone else can have what nature shows at her best."

Some people are at their best when things are at their worst.

Lori Peterson practices law in Minneapolis. I read an article about her in one of our alternative newspapers and I thought she might belong in this book. It was worth a try, anyway. So I called. Immediately, I knew I was right. I scarcely had a chance to tell her how impressed I had been with the smashing article, and that I hoped she wouldn't mind answering a few questions, as I love to study successful people, when ... "Excuse me," she said, "but before we get into the conversation, would you be available for lunch next week?"

I couldn't believe it. I hadn't known her thirty seconds and she had already grabbed the steering wheel.

"Why?"

Without missing a beat, she said, "Well, I think I recognize an unusual opportunity here to raise some money for one of my favorite charities called Adopt-A-Pet, and I could do it much better in person."

Do I know how to pick 'em? This lawyer turns out to be the consummate salesperson, instantly going into action, putting the touch on another peddler. I was about to leave town, so we put lunch on hold, but I was able to get her to tell me how she got such a fast start on life right out of the blocks.

She is from the farming community of Hawley, Minnesota. I can best describe the location as about twenty miles east of the North Dakota border on Highway 10, but I'm not sure that helps any. Her parents are schoolteachers. She got turned on by politics when she was twelve years old, by, of all people, Jimmy Carter, who must have exhausted his entire supply of charisma on Peterson. Since she met him in Plains, Georgia, she has kept in touch with the former president and Rosalyn Carter with an exchange of letters, small gifts, and visits throughout the years.

She's twenty-eight now, only two years out of law school at the University of Minnesota, and until this year, practicing on her own. No fancy degree or high-powered law firm to indulge her in her political and social concerns.

Her personal life is surprisingly conventional. She's

married to a man she met in college. They've been together ten years.

Then, there's her appearance. When she appeared on one TV show, at first the producers thought she was there as a member of the Stroh's Beer Swedish Bikini Team. Instead, Peterson was on the show to discuss her lawsuit against Stroh's on behalf of eight women employed in the brewery's St. Paul plant who were charging sexual harassment.

As for the Swedish Bikini Team, Stroh's fictional airhead blonde bimbo group, Stroh's eventually announced that the campaign was being withdrawn. And, of course, they denied that Peterson's criticism that the promotion was indicative of the company's insensitivity to women had anything to do with their decision. A master of timing, Peterson had taken on the harassment cases in April but launched her public campaign against Stroh's three weeks after the Thomas-Hill hearings.

In other less skilled, more conventional hands, the Stroh's matter could have been just another lawsuit, quietly settled between members of the Old Boys Club. In Peterson's hands, the lawyer's arsenal in sexual harassment cases has just been upgraded to include a brand new high-tech weapons system. Peterson has appeared on more than forty TV news and talk shows and on dozens of radio call-in programs in addition to being interviewed by the *Wall Street Journal,* the *Washington Post,* the *New York Times,* and scores of other papers.

She's earned a liberal battle ribbon for being scolded by national conservative columnist George Will. But, to confound liberal purists, she doesn't apologize for being financially successful as well. A jet black Jaguar XJS purrs gently at her command. But Jaguar or not, "Whenever I get a big check, my husband and I have an agreement that I give the first ten percent to animal shelters."

I have the feeling that our area is going to have some of the best cared for mutts in the country.

Some people defy every attempt to pigeonhole them. They succeed because they refuse to conform to preconceived notions, because they're constantly being underestimated, because they don't wait around for someone to tap them with a magic wand, because they have the talent and guts to break the mold. Lori Peterson is one of them. Like Mike Brewer, they're hard to spot, but great people to know and to hire, too.

56

HOW I GOT THE JOB I WANTED, #7

I got retained *on salary* in my current company with no experience other than two weeks of moderately successful commission sales by doing the following thing which outraged my wife:

I knew the commission sales scheme was hopeless: I was to enroll students in May, June, and July to begin business training at a college several hundred miles away in the fall. For each enrollment I sent in I would receive a commission of $125. If the student didn't start school (which is not uncommon in this business) I'd be charged back the $125 in the fall.

When I'd collected a few hundred dollars in commissions I realized the whole thing was not for me. So I wrote a letter of resignation to the vice-president who hired me praising the company for giving me a chance to earn such generous commissions, and regretting that I could not devote my full efforts to this sales opportunity. But the main feature of my letter was this: I enclosed a signed blank check marked "not to exceed $600," explaining that this check would cover any charge-backs I might incur as a result of no-starts in the fall.

Much to the surprise of my wife, who couldn't understand what I was doing in blithely sending off a much-needed six hundred dollars, the vice-president of the company was so impressed with my honesty and integrity, he offered me a salaried job on the spot. I have had numerous positions with the company since then, and they have always regarded me as someone with a track record for proven and documented honesty. Happily, my value system squared with the company's. The check was never cashed.

Gary Kolar
Atlanta, Georgia

(Mr. Kolar is director of marketing for a large chain of private colleges.)

57

THE OCTOPUS EXERCISE

As I mentioned earlier, during the course of a lifetime, you're likely not only to make 10.3 job changes but also five *career* changes. By my lightning calculations, it appears that for every two times you change jobs, you're also going to change careers.

Take a sheet of paper.

Draw a small circle in the center.

That's the body of the octopus.

That also represents the skills and knowledge you use in your present job or in your most recent job. It's the controlling mechanism over your drive to reach out and grab onto other jobs.

Now draw a series of lines branching out from that central area. These represent jobs different from the one you have now, but jobs for which you could conceivably be qualified if you had to shift careers.

For instance, let's say you're the rental agent for a major real estate firm in your town. You've been at the business for five years, and your general knowledge of commercial real estate is pretty good. What other jobs could you reach out for?

How about site locator for a major retailer?

Negotiator?

Physical plant and property manager for a major manufacturer?

Real estate auditor for an investment trust?

Rental investigator for a municipal or taxing authority?

Manager of real estate and construction for your local college?

Instructor in commercial real estate at the college?

Appraiser for a local bank or housing authority?

That's eight arms. If you're knowledgeable in commercial real estate, you could probably build an octopus with eighteen arms. Here are some real-life octopi:

• Nancy Chrysler, a journalist, was at the top of her profession as a reporter for the *New York Times,* the nation's leading newspaper. At forty-eight, she asked herself the inevitable question of forty-eight-year-olds everywhere, "Is this all there is?" Apparently not, so she chucked it all. As a reporter, she had gone out on assignment with photographers for years but never worked professionally as one. Using her training in photography from Columbia University's School of Journalism and her reporter's skills as an observer, she sidestepped from depicting events verbally to depicting them visually.

She is now a nature photographer in Naples, Florida.

•   Sheila Cook, an unemployed, divorced housewife´ with limited financial resources, used her homemaker's skills to advantage to found Cook's Classics, a Mountain Valley, California, manufacturer of low-sodium, low-cholesterol, low-fat salad dressings.

•   Jerry Stoffers thought he would wind down from his wartime experiences in Vietnam with a no-brain job as a gofer, hauling ceramic pots from Mexico to Los Angeles street merchants. Today, he's the head of a ten million-dollar importing business, and his employees are doing the heavy work. He used his skills to grab a higher rung of the ladder in a do-it-yourself, classically entrepreneurial profession.

•   While the octopus exercise works best if you reach up or reach sideways, it usually doesn't pay to reach down. An out-of-work broadcast sales manager couldn't land an interview with other sales managers when he reached down to apply for straight sales jobs. Sales managers saw him as a threat to grab their jobs. And he was. He repositioned himself to reach up and contacted station owners for a job as a station manager. Eventually he was hired.

•   Even corporations have learned to wean themselves away from old, dying careers and move on to new ones. Just a few years ago, Hughes Aircraft was building military hardware to thwart the ambitions of the Evil Empire. Today, they're moving into designing electric cars to position themselves for the trend toward antipollutant, environmentally sound vehicles. The president of Hughes, C. Michael Armstrong, fits the pattern himself. He had been a senior vice-president at IBM and was thought to be the heir apparent to the president's job when he switched industries to head up Hughes.

•   And now for the octopus with the biggest reach of

all. After serving nine years in prison, Bruce Perlowin became national sales manager of an import company. In his resume he cited references in magazine articles to his "formidable management skills" and "organizational genius" as a marijuana dealer and tax evader to help land the job.

58

SORRY, BUT THIS PHONE HAS BEEN PERMANENTLY DISCONNECTED

Working for the phone company used to be regarded as the closest thing there was to civil service. No one ever got fired, everyone was a lifer, and if you worked there long enough you were said to develop a bell-shaped head.

Just as an example of how things have changed in our economy over the past few years, US West, one of the seven Baby Bells created by the breakup of AT&T, announced shortly before the beginning of 1992 that six thousand people would be affected by a downsizing of their fourteen-state operation.

For the five hundred people of the Management Ser-

---

vice Organization Department, located in Minneapolis, it meant that 30 percent of them would be gone.

It had never happened before.

But since it had happened, the next question was, who would be released? The textbook method for making the layoffs would be for managers to rate and rank the people under their supervision and prune the tree accordingly.

But not much goes down that paint-by-the-numbers road anymore.

Instead, MSO employees were told that all the positions in the department were to be considered open and unfilled. Anyone who wanted to stay with the company would have to start from scratch and reapply for a job, their own job or, if they wanted to, anyone else's job in the department. If you didn't make an application, you had up to ninety days to find a new position in another department. Failing that you received a termination package.

If you decided you wanted a job, first you filled out a form, supplying a targeted written resume.

What's a targeted resume? Well, there's the normal stuff about background, experience, and qualifications, but it also calls for accurate and specific responses to questions about job requirements. For example, if the job you were applying for called for "analytic competency," you had better say you have "analytic competency" and list accomplishments that demonstrate "analytic competency," and not just say you "can do analysis."

If you did make the first cut, you were then interviewed by a higher management team. If your own job was one of the jobs you were applying for, one member of that team was always your present boss, making it a bit tough to fudge on "accomplishments."

Now look at these interview questions for the pricing/cost analyst position. It doesn't matter how many people you've supervised. There's no emphasis on "responsibilities." The model is strictly outcome-oriented. Results are what count. You're given problems to solve, and you had better be fast enough on your feet to solve them. We'll skip the early, technical questions (2a, b, c) that only an experienced cost analyst would be trained to handle. It starts getting interesting at question 3. Here goes:

This will be a situational interview. Please be specific and provide recent information as answers to my questions. I will be taking notes to document accurately the information you provide in response to the questions. There will be time at the end of the interview for questions.

1a. List your job preferences for which you are being interviewed.

1) _____

2) _____

1b. The Pricing/Costing Analyst jobs are location specific with regard to quantity and area of expertise. There is no budget for relocation. Are you willing to relocate at your own expense? (You may specify no or specify by job location.)

1c. This is a full-time position, forty hours and five days per week. Work hours are generally between 8:00 a.m. and 5:00 p.m. with some flexibility on start and stop times. The job also requires occasional overtime on short notice. Are these requirements you can meet for this position?

No _____ (A "no" answer terminates the interview)

Yes _____

3a. Think of a situation in which you and a client had differing perceptions of what needed to be done. Describe the situation. What action did you take? What was the outcome?

Situation

Action

Result

3b. Describe a situation in your job where you had a number of deadlines to be met at the same time. How did you handle that? What was the result?

Situation

Action

Result

Customer/Client Focus Questions

3c. How have you reacted to a client's request to rearrange or otherwise change cost and/or price results? Describe the situation. How did you handle it? What was the result?

Situation

Action

Result

If you have ever refused to make such a change, give an example of the situation.

General Focus Questions

4a. What have you done recently to create a sense of team and teamwork both within and outside your work-group? Describe what you did.

What were the results?

Within the group:

Situation

Action

Result

Outside the group:

Situation

Action

Result

4b. Give an example of a situation in which you took responsibility and got the job done, even though it wasn't clearly yours. Describe the situation. What actions did you take? What were the results? Why did you do it?

Situation

Action

Result

End of interview. End of job?

Recognizing that the time had come to shake its monopoly image and adopt a lean, mean competitive stance, US West determined that the way to do it was to keep its best people, but *only* its best people. If it can happen at Ma Bell's house, then anyone, anywhere, anytime can be laid off. Are you prepared to reapply for your own job? Is someone in your firm better prepared to do it than you are?

Does the bell toll for thee?

59

THERE'S MORE TO GETTING AN EDUCA-TION THAN GETTING AN EDUCATION

I'll never quit telling you that education is vital to keeping and holding a job. There's also a side benefit to school that seldom gets mentioned: the value of the placement service. Before you decide where you're going to school or going back to school, make sure you check with alums to see how helpful the school, or someone connected with it, was in preparing them for finding a job. Given the tightened job market and the increased emphasis on education for career preparation rather than for its own sake, some schools have really gotten with the program.

Barry Merkin was formerly the CEO of Dresher, Incorporated, a once ailing business that he transformed into the nation's largest manufacturer of brass beds. Now he's executive in residence and director of special programs at DePaul University in Chicago, one of the largest Catholic universities in the country, with the second largest MBA program among all the nation's universities. I've known Barry for over twenty years, traveled around the world with him, and learned just this spring that he'd been named by students as the outstanding teacher in the business program during his first year as a prof. Like getting the MVP award your rookie year … without having played in the minors!

What makes his classes so outstanding? The title of his course provides part of the answer: "Motorola On Site: A Study of Ideas." Barry uses the analogy of training an airline pilot: "Many hours are required in a flight simulator. Over and over, numerous changes are simulated, such as storms, power failure, and air traffic. It is imperative to gain as many flying skills as possible before getting into the air." The course work is done entirely off-campus, at the Motorola Museum, with a hands-on approach to business problems, combining practical experience and analysis. No formal textbook, no lectures, no memorization. Instead, interpersonal skills and problem-solving ability are the tools for success. Just like the real world.

The *New York Times* reports that Susquehanna University has begun a mentorship program for women students that begins in their freshman year in business school and continues through graduation. Each student is assigned an alumna of the school who has been successful in business. They include executives at major corporations like Quaker Oats, Citicorp, and Equitable Life.

At Texas A&M last year, over seven thousand freshmen and sophomores were expected to enroll in "Reality 101," which emphasizes the need for people skills, writing skills, and developing a job history through summer employment. Dr. C. Wayne Terrell, the university's acting director of career planning, said he wants the seminars to have "almost a shock effect on students."

There is still no substitute for an instructor who takes a personal interest in your future. In semitrade disciplines like graphic arts and journalism, the recommendation of the right professor is the key to a job. Many of these faculty members originally came from the private sector and maintain their contacts there for their entire teaching careers. They pride themselves on placing "their" students on the fast track, and it's not unusual for several generations of students who were considered disciples of the same professor to be heavily represented in a single corporation. In fact, some companies have such confidence in certain instructors that they'll call the campus every spring and ask, "Who have you got for me this year?" Get an "in" with the prof and your name could be the answer to that question.

I have made my own informal survey on the subject of schools that practice innovative learning techniques. It's not uncommon for me, as an author of business books, to field requests to speak to business students.

Professor Lilith Haynes of Babson College in Massachusetts has a career selling envelopes waiting for her if she ever decides to quit teaching. When she called, I had to turn down a speaking engagement to her class of thirty marketing students because of a travel commitment. My "no" just caused her, like any good marketing pro, to shift gears and accelerate. "Well, I certainly understand, so let's talk about Plan B for a minute. Since you can't be here, would you consider talking to the class over the phone? We'll set up a speaker phone so the entire class can engage. It will be approximately a two-hour session and this way every student can ask you a well-thought-out, substantive, in-depth question on your books, the books we have all been studying so hard this past semester." In phone jargon, this group talk thing is referred to as tele-conferencing. Professor Haynes delicately refrained from jarring the ears of this envelope manufacturer with the kind of unnecessary buzzwords my electronic competitors seem to favor. Oh well, I suppose asking them to mail in their questions would be a bit much.

"Okay, I'm game," I said. So for two hours they pummeled me. Very bright. Very good questions. Many of them career-oriented. It's no wonder Babson was named the nation's top business specialty school for three consecutive years by *U.S. News and World Report*. I hope every teaching professional reading this book will copy Haynes's idea and bring the business community to the classroom. (But please, don't all call me! I'll be happy to furnish you with Tom Peters's number.)

60

NO ISN'T AN ANSWER... IT'S A QUESTION

Two guys are facing the firing squad. The officer in charge has just finished "Ready! Aim!" and is on the verge of "Fire!" when one of the men about to be shot yells, "Hey, wait a minute. First of all, this blindfold's too tight; second, you didn't offer us a last cigarette; and third, I should get a chance to say a few words, like 'Long live the Revolution' and things like that."

"Shhh," says the other guy. "Don't make trouble."

What do we do when the game is lost? We sulk. We pout. We grouse. We sow sour grapes. When we've lost out in a job search, it's "How could that dumb company be so dumb to hire that other dumb guy instead of me?"

Hey, that's human nature. The only people I know

who smile and hug the winner when they've lost are the forty-nine non–Miss Americas in the annual Miss America pageant. And a gentleman I'll call Carl Hernandez.

Carl is an electrical engineer in Spokane who specializes in aeronautics. I met him playing tennis in Arizona. He knows his ohms and amps just as well as his lobs and aces, but like millions of others over the last few years, he spent a long, long time on the bench between jobs. One evening, over quesadillas and Coronas, Carl told me how he managed to get a new job with a defense contractor during the period of the worst cutbacks and layoffs in industry history.

Three times Carl was among the twenty to thirty contenders for a plum position. Three times the jobs went to others instead of to him.

"Finally, I got smart," said Carl. "What did I do in lab in school when an experiment didn't work? I tried to figure out what went wrong. I examined the materials. I checked the measurements. I reread my notes. And when I couldn't figure out why I was messing up, I buddied up to one of the people who seemed to be doing it right."

After Carl lost out on a job for the third time, he found out the names of the persons who had beaten him out the last two times and wrote them each a note. It went like this:

> Congratulations on your new appointment! Your firm is lucky to have you, and I'm sure you're going to knock 'em dead on your new assignment.
>
> I was also a candidate for the job for which you were hired. I'd be less than honest if I didn't admit it was a disappointment not to be selected; but your new firm is a great company, and it doesn't make mistakes in hiring decisions as important as this one.
>
> I'd like to ask you a special favor. Would you let me take you to lunch so I can learn a bit more about

you and what made you so successful in a tough job market? Given our specialty, we've both been trained to learn by observation, and to expand our pools of knowledge by sharing what we've learned. That's what I hope to do. I'll be calling you soon to see if it's possible to set up an appointment.

In his phone calls, Carl was able to overcome the initial suspicion that the letter set off. Both of the lunches were worth their weight in Whartons.

After both the meetings, Carl ran to find a place as soon as possible where he could sit down, make notes, and give himself a thorough debriefing as soon as possible. He didn't want to forget even the smallest detail: How they answered questions, how they dressed, what their goals were, their educational and career experience, what they emphasized and deemphasized. He followed up with a thank-you note, and he took what he had learned to fine-tune his own presentation and bring it into line with what the marketplace was buying.

In his first interview after his meetings, with the right attitude and the current buzz straight from the winners' circle, Carl landed the job he holds today.

Why did this approach work when his attempts to find out from the companies that had turned him down netted nothing useful? Because the firms that don't hire you will *never* give you a straight answer. They're afraid, and not without some sad experiences along these lines, that telling you "we thought your answers were evasive," or "your personal style seems incompatible with the boss you'd be working for" would expose them to the possibility of litigation or, at best, bad PR. But it's a different story when you talk to a successful job candidate. It's as impossible for the new hiree not to tell you why he got the job as it is for a Lotto winner not to tell you how he picked the winning numbers.

Who's more likely to open up to you, someone with a natural interest in concealing the truth, or someone with a natural desire to give you the insider's scoop?

If second place only counts in horseshoes, this is horseshoes.

Here's the way to stand the conventional wisdom on its head and prove that second is not last and that runners-up are not also-rans ... they finish in the money. Didn't get the job? Just a blip on the screen. American lives don't have second acts? Just make the effort to turn the page and you can write your own happy ending.

Whatever we're trying to learn, whatever talent we're trying to develop, whatever skill we're trying to improve, whether it's sports, speaking ability, selling technique, we learn by watching the experts. Is it all in the wrist? Look closely enough and you can see for yourself. Every job you *didn't* get, someone else did. There's your expert.

Observe.

Learn.

Use this technique and you can convert a turndown into a thumbs-up.

61

INSIDE EVERY 98 LB. WEAKLING IS A CHARLES ATLAS TRYING TO GET OUT

When I was a kid, the back of every comic book had an advertisement for a body-building course being sold by a character who called himself Charles Atlas. The pitch was done in comic strip fashion. It opened with a panel showing a puny adolescent at the beach with his foxy girl-friend. Along comes a monster bully. He kicks sand in the skinny kid's face and strides off with the lady. The scene shifts. Our hero, now alone in his room, is desperate to avenge his humiliation. He sees Atlas's ad in a magazine and mails in the coupon. Soon, the Dynamic Tension course arrives. After a few easy workouts, he is trans-formed into hunkdom. He goes back to the beach, fearlessly escalates matters from sand-kicking to duking out his rival, wins back his flighty girlfriend, and, if I recall correctly, draws admiring glances from other beach bunnies.

What makes the whole thing work—and it really did work; the same ad ran unchanged for decades—is that the weight of the argument for the muscle course falls on the joy of getting even. Is our hero beefing up to prove his love for the girl? Hardly. In fact, the last panel suggests he has some getting even to do with her, too. He and his now bulging pectorals can move on to greener pastures anytime he feels like it.

The Atlas approach hasn't changed a whit since my adolescent daydreams of Schwarzenegger-like dominion over the known world.

That's because it still works.

In the hands of a master, this wad of bubble-gum psychology is as effective a tool as you can deploy.

Bob Knight, Indiana basketball coach, will never win any popularity contests with his players. He curses them. He rages. And they respond. They know they're good. They live to prove that the arrogant, overbearing, all-knowing Knight is wrong, wrong, wrong. He lives to let them prove it.

You'll never hear Knight knock his opponents. That's different. He knows the real purpose of cutting comments. Any slighting remark he made against another team would be plastered immediately on his rivals' locker-room bulletin boards to inspire them to greater efforts against him.

The oldest cliché in sports is that nothing generates a superior performance more than the chance to prove to the world that the guy who traded you away was an idiot. One of my favorite examples is a boyhood hero named Larry Rosenthal, who made his way from the St. Paul sandlots through the minors and eventually to the bigs, where he was an American League outfielder for eight years. In 1944, Larry was with the Yankees, who, as usual in those days, were in the thick of the pennant race. Midway through the season the Yankees traded Larry, and his chance for a World Series check, to the lowly Philadelphia Athletics. Sure enough, it was his late-season, ninth-inning homer for the A's that knocked the Yankees out of contention and gave the pennant for the first and only time to the St. Louis Browns.

Larry died at age eighty-one in March of 1992. He had had a long and productive life. The baseball years were just a tiny fraction of that life, and the one swing of the bat he never tired of recalling was the tiniest fraction of that fraction. Just one at-bat nearly fifty years ago, and it was the centerpiece of his life, the centerpiece of his obituary. I can almost write the headline describing Larry's big game: SCORNED PLAYER GETS EVEN WITH MIGHTY YANKEES.

Revenge is more than an emotion; it can become an obsession.

I know.

When I went through the big brouhaha to help get state financing for the domed stadium in Minneapolis that would keep the Minnesota Twins, the professional baseball team, and the Minnesota Vikings, the professional football team, in our area, I not only gained first-hand knowledge of what politics was really like, I also learned what it was like to acquire a mortal enemy.

Because I was chairman of the Stadium Task Force, I was very visible throughout the whole process. I drew my share of ink, some friendly, some not so friendly. That comes with the territory. When you take a public position on a controversial issue, you have to expect some flak. But I had drawn the Death Card. Doctor Doom. The Queen of Spades. Go Directly to Jail. The Hangman. My antagonist, a local sports columnist named Pat Reusse, did not just disagree with me. He was at war with me. To him, I was not even just your average sports nut and business boob trying to get some dough from the public trough for a nutty pet project. I had come to earth to blot out the sun, to loot and pillage, and to sentence millions of meek, innocent, working stiffs to lifetimes of grinding poverty and dimly lit sports events. All just so I could sit in an air-conditioned box, insulated from the true sports fans, and quaff Chablis while I watched dumb jocks bang heads.

He didn't much care for me.

To make matters worse, he was and still is a very clever, very funny writer, with a great talent for invective. Knowing I couldn't fight him on his terms, I fought him on mine. I was turtle to his hare. I doggedly pursued my dream, year after year, session after session. As every legislative session wheezed to its constitutionally commanded final moments, blankets were thrown over the clocks in the House and Senate chambers. A reminder, as if one were needed, that we were totally immersed in the fantasy world of politics, where only clocks can be trusted to tell the truth, and are covered up for doing just that. And year after year, session after session, my nemesis, Reusse, continued to dog me at every turn of the road.

At one point, our twenty-eight-person task force took a vote on whether to disband: Twenty-five voted in favor of going for the life rafts and abandoning ship, after first throwing the captain overboard. I would have quit then and there, if the vision of Reusse's leering face, laughing at my failure, hadn't danced before my eyes.

As if the vision of my leering face, laughing at his, hadn't given me an even more compelling reason to keep at it.

So, thanks to Reusse, we finally got funded and the Hubert H. Humphrey Metrodome was built.

I fantasized for years about the moment when I would

finally cross home plate, when I would get to throw out the first ball at the opening-day ceremonies.

What I failed to mention was that, in my mind's eye, I was throwing it right at the tenderest part of Pat Reusse's overinflated ego.

That should have put an end to it, but it didn't. No matter what I was involved in after that (recruiting Lou Holtz to coach the University of Minnesota football team; organizing the ticket-buyout campaign to keep the Twins from moving to Florida; waging the long battle to stage the 1992 Super Bowl in the Hubert H. Humphrey Metrodome; helping us win an NBA franchise; keeping the North Stars in Minnesota), Reusse was always there with his scorecard, reading, "Mackay: 0; Rest of World: 117, and still in possession of the ball."

The man had a way of making me simply salivate to stay in the game, just so he'd have to think up new ways to say why I didn't belong there.

So you got fired.

You can take the hurt and anger you feel and use it constructively. To prove they made a mistake when they let you go. Think. And do. Prove those critics wrong, wrong, wrong. Keep the vision of their pinched little faces handy, where you can get at them when you need them. Make them eat their words. Show them your stuff. Get mad. Get going. Get even.

Payback time is coming.

62

HOW TO NEGOTIATE ON THE OFF CHANCE THAT YOU'RE NOT BOB HOPE

One of the many glitches in the human makeup is the difference in our abilities when it comes to performing for others as compared to how we perform for ourselves. It always zonks me out to read about the psychiatrist who has helped so many of his patients rebuild their lives but whose own personal life is in turmoil, or the financial adviser who never picked a stock right for himself but managed to build a tidy pile for his clients.

Not many of us are able to do things for ourselves the same way we do them for others, whether that translates into being better at our jobs or better at our own affairs. Even people who make their livings negotiating may not maximize the use of their professional skills to advance their own personal interests. Not every real estate expert who spends his career negotiating shopping center leases is an expert when it comes to negotiating his own raise. The insurance company adjuster who knocks heads all day long negotiating settlements with personal injury lawyers still may be a patsy in settling his own salary differences with his employer.

Unfortunately, there's no way we can escape having to represent our own interests, whether we're good at it or not. So we might as well try to learn how to be good at it. Whether or not you've ever negotiated anything else in your life, when it comes to getting a job, asking for a promotion or a raise, or even hanging onto the job you have, at some time your ability to negotiate on your own behalf is going to be tested.

Bob Hope probably made more money in California real estate than he did in entertainment. His name periodically pops up on lists of the five hundred or the thousand richest Americans. Hope's legendary success as a businessman has been attributed to his oft-quoted advice: "Go out to where the houses end and start buying land."

That helps—a little—but there's a bit more to it. Where the houses currently end is not always where the new development begins.

You need superior information. If you're Bob Hope, you can probably drop a few one-liners and get the planning department or the city council to tip you off on what the zoning map is going to look like five years from now. If you're not that funny or famous, you may have to spend a lot of time, money, and effort to get a sense of where the powers that be are going to wave their magic rezoning wand. Don't buy raw land because the community just "has" to grow in the direction of your acreage. It doesn't have to grow anywhere unless the powers that be say it has to.

You also need staying power. The more time it takes for raw land to be developed, the more money it devours. Non–income-producing real estate is a cesspool for money. Even when superior information tells you where the growth is going to occur, approvals and clearances and permits and licenses and taxes and fees and actual construction take longer and cost more than you ever dreamed possible. And, oh yes, banks have been known to change their minds, and there goes the financing.

But still, what you need most of all in order to survive is negotiating skill. You don't get rich just buying land. You have to be skilled in knowing how much to pay for it. You have to be skilled in *selling* it, too.

One of the common misunderstandings about negotiating is that it is a kind of sophisticated way of resolving a conflict. If you are able to present better, more reasoned arguments than your negotiating opponent, you're likely to win.

"Useless nonsense," says Dr. George Mascioszek, a German business consultant. "Someone who wants to sell his business can hardly be convinced that five million dollars would be better for them than six million." Good arguments do not help deuces beat aces at the card table. Wars are not won by the nations with the strongest oral arguments. When you buy a car, how badly you need and deserve one doesn't have much bearing on how much you pay for it. Sweet reason occasionally wins in a courtroom, but people who hire lawyers as business negotiators are applying a fine instrument where a blunt one is called for.

What decides a negotiation? Mascioszek's answer: "People seek incentives and flee punishment, avoiding punishment being the stronger incentive. Someone who is about to lose his job will be fully awake and do his best to avert the loss, while someone who is told of an opportunity to double his income will not normally rush into action."

One way Bob Hope was able to win his negotiations was by keeping his opponents off balance. If they had not met him and had "bought the act"—in other words, if they thought he was the same jovial airhead in the flesh as he was when he was performing—he could seem cold and taciturn, concealing clues as to his true motives, his best price. Hope knew how to let their imaginations create their own worst-case scenario ... if they pushed him, he would walk, and their dreams of dining out for the next twenty years on their "I-did-business-with-Bob-Hope" story would vanish.

He had a two-word script for his negotiations. When he was approached by a seller, it was "too much." When he was approached by a buyer, it was "too little."

The performance was so unexpected and convincing that his negotiating opponents usually decided that if they wanted to deal with him it would be on his terms. It usually was. Bob Hope has always been a world-class negotiator because he is a world-class performer in every sense of the word. And because he did his homework. He *knew* the value of what he was buying or selling.

Whatever you're negotiating for, including a job, you'll do best if you forget the flowery speeches and concentrate on knowing your opponent's strengths and weaknesses.

Is time your enemy or your ally? Will you get a better price by stalling or by pushing the deal to completion? Who is the most experienced? Who knows the most about the value of the specific property or service that is being offered for sale? Who is better able to predict its future value?

Who's tipping his or her hand and giving the opponent the clues to their true motive? The true price?

Who has the most to lose if the deal doesn't go through? Who is best able to convince his or her opponent that he or she can walk away from the deal and never look back?

The longer you've been at it and the more you know, the better your negotiating position.

Car dealers win in negotiations because they have superior information. They know exactly how much they paid for the car they are trying to sell, and because they are so experienced in evaluating cars, they also know exactly, well, almost exactly, how much the trade-in you're offering is worth. Few ordinary car buyers are well-informed enough to know those two critical numbers. And even when they think they do, the dealer throws in variables like options and financing charges that help disguise the dealership's true margin of profit. The result is that only the most sophisticated customers know how to cut a deal without cutting their own throats. Among dealers, the good ones are so good at it, they can conceal their own skill. The true pro has the customer believing he or she has stolen the car.

The secret of negotiating? Silence is golden. Be like Bob Hope. Do as little negotiating as possible. Know the answer to every question you might be asked *before* you sit down at the table and you won't have to appear as if you are negotiating.

Al, a friend of mine, went to his annual performance review knowing that he had done an excellent job during the preceding year but concerned that his personal performance would be offset by the company's less than stellar results during the recession. Armed with statistics and kudos from his supervisor, he was hoping for a 10 percent raise.

When Al got into the boss's office, he sat there stone-faced, listening to the boss recite the company line, finally winding up the litany of woes with his offer.

"Al, the best we can do this year is a fifteen percent increase."

"I was so dumbfounded, I didn't know what the hell to say," Al told me. "So I didn't say anything. That's when the boss said, 'All right, we'll make it twenty-five percent.' I wonder, if I hadn't finally managed to choke out a 'thank you,' would he have made it thirty-five percent?"

Pounding the table only works in the movies. Skilled negotiators like Bob Hope have been in enough movies to know that it's different in real life.

Don't make decisions for people. When you let them decide, you *make* them decide.

Stay calm. If you're tight in the batter's box, you can't hit. The high average hitters always keep a quiet bat until it's time to swing.

If you're setting or resetting a salary for a job, you must be able to evaluate yourself, your negotiating opponent, and your negotiating position realistically.

Why were you offered the job in the first place? Experience? Skills? Education? Do you fit the profile of the ideal candidate, or does it seem that the person or company hiring you is just going to try you on for size? Do you know how much the job is worth in the marketplace? What perks the company might be willing to include?

As a tactical matter, always try to have your bargaining opponent make the first offer. You never know; it can be a pleasant surprise. On the other hand, if you make the first offer and suggest a number lower than the employer was about to offer you, you're giving the other side a pleasant surprise ... and that's not the object of the exercise. Try to finesse the "What do you need for a salary" question with "Do you have a salary range established for this position?"

Evaluate the employer. What do you know about their needs? Is this a tough position to fill? Do they have the reputation for being high payers or low payers? Are they noted for high or low turnover? Do they tend to provide a fast track or a slow track for their employees?

Evaluate yourself. What bargaining advantage do you

hold? Top grades? Great potential? Superior past performance? First-rate credentials and experience? Proven skills? Proven loyalty? Will it matter to the company if they don't hire you and hire someone else instead? Is your potential to perform of such value to them that they wouldn't want it to go to a competitor? Can you prove it?

This is the kind of information that's vital in winning the negotiation for a job or an advancement. You don't present it as an "argument." It's the knowledge and composure you carry with you to the table that gives you a competitive edge in any negotiation.

63

BEFORE YOU TAKE THE JOB THEY *OFFER*, OFFER TO TAKE THE JOB YOU *WANT*

Now let's move our discussion of negotiating from the general to the specific. The clouds part. The sun shines. You've been offered the job. The brief, beautiful moment in which you can cut the best deal possible for yourself has arrived.

What now?

First of all, return to earth. Don't let the euphoria of the moment cloud your judgment. If a recruiter is involved, remember, recruiters work for the company, not for you. Resist the impulse to prostrate yourself at his or her feet. They know how to make the most of that reaction, and it won't work in your favor. You're happy. Not ecstatic. Next, let's get real. Unless you can run a 3.4 forty and throw a football sixty-five yards, you're at a disadvantage.

Most of the time recruiters don't come knocking on your door. You knock on theirs. They know you're panting for the job.

From your point of view, the key is to look at *all* the elements of the package *compared* to your needs.

Now hold that thought: "All" and "compared to your needs" are genuine biggies.

The "all" idea is to eliminate any surprises and disappointments once the marriage is under way. You need to know as much as possible before you sign on. Once you accept the job, there isn't anything left to talk about. You can't negotiate anything after you've agreed to it.

You're in the army now.

"Oh, didn't you know our executives are always expected to turn in time sheets every day?" and "We never, ever allow our people to rent anything but an economy car on the road" and "It's not company policy to allow severance pay unless we agreed to a severance package with you *before* you were hired. Do you have anything in writing?"

These are not the words you want to hear after you've agreed to take the job.

You must have had a few clues that you might be hired before the golden moment occurred. That was the time to do some planning, to think of what to ask about, to have in mind what concessions you'd be willing to make to accept the company's offer.

We'll get to your list in a moment, but before we do, remember, be careful about appearing to be too hard-nosed. You're polite, smiling, and, at this point, just seeking information. Usually, for management jobs, it takes several discussions to nail down the details and generate a written offer letter.

Now here's the list. The key points that should be covered include:

Salary (and how often it will be renegotiated)
Bonuses and bonus guarantees
Vacation, sick leave, and personal time
Hours of work
Records and reports required
Pension and pension vesting rights
Savings plans and stock options
Medical coverage and other benefits
Relocation package
Compensation and performance review cycle
Title and reporting relationships
Performance expectations
Social obligations and expectations
Community involvement requirements and expecta-
    tions
Training programs
Advancement and promotion opportunities
Expense allowances
Travel requirements
Severance terms

Any other special duties the company expects you to perform. (Does the last hire always have to play the Easter Bunny at the annual egg roll?)

Make careful notes during these discussions, and be aware of any slippage as the preliminary talks proceed. It's not uncommon for companies to try to short-sheet candidates they think are really interested in the job or to promise one thing orally and another in writing. Confirm conversations in writing as soon as possible.

Don't accept the offer until you've covered *all*—there's

that word again—the topics on your list. That's the best single way there is to maximize your package.

Don't forget, the secret of negotiating is to negotiate as little as possible. You try to get as much information as you can from the other side while providing minimal information from your side.

Keep that smile working, and if the company starts to backslide, consult your notes and remind them, ever so gently, of what you *thought* you heard before and what you carefully wrote down.

Once you've got the offer, the whole offer, on the table, ready to commit to writing, you're now in a position to discuss the "compared to your needs" part of the equation. This is when you can do some negotiating in the traditional sense. Every company has its own quirky little policies. And so do you.

Some firms haven't bothered to update their day care policies; but it could be a major concern to you. Knowing the trend toward day care, you might be able to achieve a breakthrough here. Would they be willing to improve the quality of their day care in any meaningful way if you would help them draft a plan?

Your last company, for example, may have provided you with a company car. This one doesn't, even though they have a substantially better pension plan. Is a compromise in order, fifty-fifty on the car?

Another area ripe for compromise is the title you'll be carrying in your new position. Conventional wisdom is: Give in on salary, give in on office size, give in on prime locker space at the executive squash courts, but never, ever give in on title.

That's badly dated advice, and it provides you with an opportunity.

There are more vice-presidents around than there are

paper clips. If you're willing to compromise on title, and you should be, you may be the answer to a personnel director's prayers. With all the downsizing and cutbacks, companies are having enormous compression problems with titles.

Consider downsizing your title as a trading card. It's your ace in the hole. Don't throw it away. Hoard it carefully and play it when you need it. It could go a long way toward helping you cut a better deal for yourself.

No matter what the outcome of the horse-trading part of the deal, by using this approach and covering every possible area of employer-employee relations you can think of in your pre-signup discussions, you're way ahead of the game, and you're way ahead of 99 percent of all hires.

64

CREAM DOESN'T RISE TO THE TOP, IT WORKS ITS WAY UP

At the advanced age of seven, I took up golf. For the next twelve years, it was my life. Every chance I got, I pounded the frozen tundra of St. Paul, Minnesota, with my sticks. In high school, I was a two-time city champion and lost the state high school championship by a stroke. I played three years of varsity golf on my college team.

As I was corralling my hundred golf trophies and reading my press clippings, the future was as clear and problem-free to me as an eighteen-inch putt. I would make my mark in the world following the sun as a golf pro. The real question was: Would I fly my own Cessna from tournament to tournament, or would I buy a Beechcraft instead?

Then I had what is known in religious circles as an epiphany. You don't see that word very often because each person gets about one a lifetime. It's a special kind of revelation, usually accompanied by something like a burning bush, or by a parting of the heavens.

Mine came at a less auspicious fork in the road: the NCAA Golf Tournament held at Purdue University in my sophomore year. Players came from colleges all over the country to compete, particularly from the southern schools, where the year-round mild climate produced the strongest golfers—players, with names unknown to me at the time, like Ken Venturi, Don January, Billy Maxwell. During that tournament, they proved they were superior to me and to the other northern players in every phase of the game.

I left Purdue in shock, my dreams forever lost in the rough.

When I got home my mother, the schoolteacher, sat me down and gave me the facts of life, of golf life, that is. She said, "Harvey, you are nineteen years old and started playing golf at age seven, which means you've been playing twelve years, probably about the same number of years as the star players you've told me about. The difference is, we live where the weather makes it impossible for you to practice much of the year. You've been playing twelve years times *five* months a year, which is sixty months total, and the top players have been playing twelve years times *twelve* months a year, which is one hundred forty-four months, or nearly two and a half times as long. Same number of years, but over twice the experience, and it's a huge chunk of time you can never make up. You don't have to be a math major to figure out that even if you have their natural talent, you'd never catch them."

In short, chalk up one retired University of Minnesota

golfer. The rest is history. The PGA's loss was the envelope industry's gain.

There are no secrets to finding a job, to keeping your present job, or to being promoted, just as there is no mystery about why Miami produces great golfers and lousy hockey players while Canada, on the other hand, produces great hockey players and a few, but just a few, decent golfers.

Just for laughs, check out the record of the Jamaican bobsled team, the joke entry in the 1992 Winter Olympics. There are good ways and bad ways, hard ways and less hard ways, but there are no real shortcuts to success.

If you're not out working harder, longer, smarter than everyone else, if you're not willing to put in the hours, stay on the job until long after the cleaning people have gone home, you can still have a good life, but you won't be living it at the top.

Edgar Bergen had Charlie McCarthy say, "Hard work never killed anyone, but why take a chance?" I say, "Don't take advice from a dummy."

When I first bought the pre–Industrial Revolution museum that eventually turned out to be Mackay Envelope, I got a cot, stuck it in the warmest corner of my "office"—a portioned-off corner on the plant floor—gave my wife a big kiss, and told her I'd see her again in two years. I see her a lot more often than that now, but she says I didn't begin coming home regularly until she told me the kids were starting to call the postman "Daddy."

Michael Jordan may make it look easy. It isn't. For years, he was out on the blacktop in Winston-Salem every day until they turned off the playground lights. Michael Jordan didn't make the team when he tried out for basketball as a high school freshman. He didn't make it either when he tried out again as a sophomore and only got rostered when another player was injured. In his junior year, he averaged a mere eleven points a game. Every step up the ladder was a struggle, but he never quit. No coach ever drove Michael Jordan as hard as he drove himself. I have a feeling that if he wanted a job and was turned down, he would still find a way eventually to wind up on the payroll.

Ross Perot, the Texas billionaire who gave Clinton and Bush a scare during the 1992 presidential campaign, presents a similar story. According to the *New York Times,* when Ross Perot was twelve years old, he decided to get a part-time job, and in the time-honored tradition of twelve-year-old boys, applied for a route with the local paper, the *Texarkana Gazette.* He was told there were no routes available. Perot pointed out that no one was delivering papers in New Town, Texarkana's worst slum. There was no market for papers there, the circulation manager insisted. Perot begged to differ and they cut a deal: Perot would develop the area in exchange for double the usual commission rate. Perot's customers proved to be much more diligent readers than the circulation manager gave them credit for, and Perot soon built the route up to the point where another time-honored American tradition was wheeled out: When the salesperson makes more money than his boss, you cut the commission. In half. Perot responded to this ploy by going over the circulation manager's head to the publisher of the paper, demanding that he honor the deal made on behalf of the *Gazette.* The paper complied.

Later, when Perot had left the navy and joined the IBM sales force, he applied the same strategy—take the tough calls—and found himself in the same situation he faced as a twelve-year-old paperboy: He was such a spectacular salesperson that one year, 1962, he had met his annual sales quota by January 19. That was the year IBM decided to change the rules in the middle of the game. Instead of paying salespeople on the basis of sales, the new formula provided for "bonuses"—at the discretion of bosses—that might or might not be paid commensurate with sales performance. That did it. With a thousand dollars borrowed from his wife, he founded Electronic Data Systems. Eight years later, his share in the company was worth $1.5 billion.

Sure, you can win the big prize ... if you'll pay the big price.

Sorry, but there just isn't any other way to get from there to here.

The good news is there will always be a place at the table for the people who are willing to work harder and longer than anyone else in the game, the people willing to take the assignments no one else wants, wrestle them to the ground, and turn them into winners.

65

IF YOU THOUGHT YOUR OLD BOSS WAS TOUGH, TRY WORKING FOR YOURSELF

I'm not much for bumper-sticker philosophy, but I saw this anonymous quotation posted on the wall of an office and I liked it so much, I thought I'd pass it on as a kind of final check-off before you stomp out the door to start your own business. Here it is:

Be thankful for the troubles of your job. They provide you with about half of your income. If it were not for the things that go wrong, the difficult people you have to deal with, the problems and unpleasantness of your working day, someone could be found to handle your job for half of what you are being paid. It takes intelligence, resourcefulness, patience, tact, and courage to meet the troubles of any job. That is why you hold your present job. And it may be the reason why you aren't holding down an even bigger one. If all of us would start to look for more troubles and learn to handle them cheerfully, and with good judgment, as opportunities rather than irritations, we would find ourselves getting ahead at a surprising rate. For it is a fact that there are plenty of jobs waiting for men and women who aren't afraid of the troubles connected with them.

Okay, you've had it with working for someone else. You've decided to start your own business. There are thousands of things to consider. Here are a few of them:

1. Think small. It is a lot cheaper, easier, and smarter to grow bigger than it is to grow smaller. Keep your overhead to a minimum by having your office at home. Hang on to your day job as long as possible or at least until you can begin to see some light at the end of the financial tunnel in your own business.

2. Get advice. Put together an outside advisory team. Find people who know how to do what you don't. You don't need advice from people who can do what you already know how to do. Keep your advisory team in place after your start-up phase is over. You won't stop making mistakes just because you've gotten bigger. You'll just make bigger ones. Remember, he who rides a tiger can't dismount.

3. Draft a business plan. You don't build a house without a blueprint. You don't take off for parts unknown without a road map. And you don't start a business without a business plan. Don't kid yourself by overestimating or wishing the numbers higher. Be realistic. In fact, don't be realistic, be pessimistic. Be a devil's advocate. Make a worst-case scenario and see if the answers still work. Don't proceed unless they do. Here are the elements you need for your plan:

- *Situation analysis.* What is your market? If your answer is "everyone," you need a new business or a new plan. What area will you serve? How many people or businesses comprise your target market? What makes you certain there are enough potential clients or consumers to support your business? Who's the competition? Why will people do business with you?

- *Financing.* Where is the money going to come from initially? Where will it come from when that runs out? Can you handle a negative cash flow? For how long? Do you have a cushion if it takes longer to become profitable than you expect? Most overnight successes in business are like overnight successes in show business ... they take years. Studies show more businesses fail because of poor management and underfinancing than for any other reasons. Don't start a business unless you have staying power. Your savings should be adequate to support you for at least two years before you have to dip into your new business for income.

- *Product analysis.* Who needs it? Why? What makes it saleable? Price? Quality? Service? Convenience? How will people learn about your product? About your business?

- *Personnel.* What talents are absolutely essential to the success of this business? Where will you find them? Have you priced their services accurately? Are you considering hiring anyone who is not totally necessary to your success? Why?

4. Be ready to adapt to change. Be prepared to handle the unexpected: an employee who doesn't perform, a product that doesn't sell. Are you flexible enough to adapt?

5. Get the details right. George Will has a great quote: "We need people who have read the minutes of the last meeting." Insurance, payroll, licenses, permits, leases, legal advice, taxes. Don't try shortcuts that can get you into trouble with the authorities.

6. It all depends on you. Do you have the temperament to work sixteen hours a day for months, or perhaps years, when things never seem to be going right? Are you prepared to work longer hours for *less* money than you ever have in any job you ever held while still maintaining traces of normal human behavior, like laughter and patience and having fun?

If so, then maybe you can handle your own business. After all, we work for dozens of reasons ... money is only one of them.

66

HOW I GOT THE JOB I WANTED, #8

In 1967, I took my first trip as a travel agent from my home in Chicago to California. Our bus passed the stadium where the Los Angeles Angels baseball team played, giving me an idea.

I loved all sports, particularly baseball. I loved travel, and most of all, I loved to organize things. Why not combine all three?

I asked the airlines representative on our tour whether we could work out a deal where they would let me use a portion of the air time they had purchased during the baseball broadcasts to promote a fans' tour on their airline, which I would then arrange.

They agreed enthusiastically.

With that support, I plunged ahead, committing for travel and hotel space and tickets to the games. What I didn't know was that a rival airline had arranged a tour from Chicago to Los Angeles for the same weekend I had been working on and they had already booked three hundred fans. To make matters worse, the airline I had been working with never ran the ads as we had agreed.

It was nearly departure date when I phoned WGN Radio, the station that broadcast the ball games, explaining my plight. The WGN executive took pity on me, very generously phoned the baseball broadcast team, and soon it was announced to the world that Phoebe Medow was escorting Chicago baseball fans to Los Angeles, and with my phone number yet! Incredible!

I took thirteen people, some retrieved from the rival airline's already closed waiting list. It was great. There we sat, all thirteen of us, fourteen counting me, our cheers for our courageous ball club nearly drowned out by the mighty three hundred-person contingent from the Grand Tour group sitting next to us.

The next year we went to Montreal, and sold out two months ahead of time with fifty-five people.

The rest is history. I opened WAY TO GO Travel Agency in the Wrigley Building. This is my twenty-fifth year of arranging and escorting sports fan tours. I've taken thousands of Cubs, White Sox, Bears, and Bulls fans to see their favorite Chicago teams on the road. I've been all over the United States and Canada. We've had twenty-four annual spring training trips, we've

seen two no-hitters, and we've even had two marriages among our fans.

Now if the Cubs would only get in the World
Series.

Phoebe Medow
Chicago, Illinois

67

WE ALL START OUT IN LIFE
WITH ONE THING IN COMMON ...

Our business, like everyone else's, is subject to the ups and downs of the economy. One of the standard gauges of economic activity is industrial paper sales, because envelopes, packaging, order forms, or any of the thousands of other kinds of office-generated paper products are always bought in quantity on an "as needed" basis, and when a recession hits, the blizzard of paper dries up. Who needs paper goods piling up in the warehouse when no one is buying the stuff it's wrapped in, no one is using order forms to write up sales, and no one is filling out purchase orders or submitting requisitions?

The pressure on salespeople to produce grows more

intense with each downward blip in the level of economic production. Sales is the engine that drives the machinery on the plant floor. Nothing happens in our shop until someone writes up an order.

During the bad times, our sales meetings take on a new urgency. The easy orders are memories. Demands for price concessions escalate like spring training batting averages. Impossible deadlines and improbable specs are standard.

Johnny Carson would have retired thirty years earlier if he'd ever had to face an audience of Mackay salespeople on a Monday morning in this kind of economic environment. When I walk in, chins are on the table, eyes are on the floor. The silence is deafening.

Then I let them have it.

"I don't care how bad business is, recession, depression, and I don't care how black and ugly the headlines are about today's economic situation. You can't let horror stories in the media become the script for your life. You have to take control of your life and not turn it over to Peter Jennings. Right now, this very minute, our competitors, Tension Envelope, Quality Park, and the rest, are writing up orders we know absolutely nothing about.

"Why? Because there are still plenty of business opportunities out there. We just haven't found them yet. We haven't looked hard enough, long enough, imaginatively enough.

"No business opportunity is ever lost. If you fumble it, your competitor will find it.

"Our competitors aren't who you think they are." Then I take off my wristwatch and hold it up. "This is our only competition. We all start out in life with one thing in common. We all have the same amount of time. It's just a matter of what we do with it.

"We've got to spend our time effectively, we've got to hustle, we've got to price better, service better, dig harder for new business, do a better job of taking care of old business. We've got to realize that no matter how tough the going is out there, it's just as tough for everyone else as it is for us. They're still in business, aren't they? They haven't quit yet. I drove by there this morning and their lights are still on and their parking lot is full. I don't see any magic envelopes coming off their machines, do you? I see them out there all the time, and they don't look, or sound, or act, a whole lot different than we do. I've never seen a Quality Park guy slip into a telephone booth and rip off his Clark Kent suit and fly off like Superman, have you? If they can do it, we can do it."

End of speech.

No one tears up the carpet rushing from the room to get out into the field, but during thirty years of roller coaster swings in the economy, I've given the same pep talk often enough to know that it works.

And it applies just as much to the unemployed and to the underemployed as it does to the envelope crowd.

Studies show that workers who tend to get the most discouraged and quit are those who are not able to make the effort to sell themselves aggressively. According to the Federal Bureau of Labor Statistics, May 1992, a million people are not just unemployed, they've abandoned the job search entirely. Apparently, they're waiting until Ted Koppel tells them times have gotten better before they start looking for a job again.

If you're one of them, just remember, while you're waiting, other people have got their heads back together, and are starting work on a new job. They're not all white, male, Harvard MBAs either. They're people just like you.

It can happen. It takes commitment. It takes believing

in yourself even when no one else does. It takes aggressive action. It takes a thick skin. It takes an endless amount of drudgery and plain, hard work. It takes a long, long time. But if someone else can do it, and, bet on it, someone else *is* doing it, every minute of the day, so can you.

68

YOU SURVIVED THE DOWNSIZE; NOW IT'S TIME TO UPSIZE: HOW TO ASK FOR A RAISE

Judging by the beaded foreheads I've seen over the last thirty years, asking for a raise can be more traumatic than the first day at the beach in a bathing suit after a long winter of hot fudge sundaes.

Whether it's shipping clerks or CEOs, the common denominator is the same: unvarnished fear.

There's a right way and a wrong way to ask for a raise. As one who has sat across the desk from armies of raise seekers over the years, I realize that describing the proper steps to take to get a raise is not the smartest thing I'll ever do in my capacity as a business owner.

But, as my publisher loves to remind me, I'm not a

---

business owner when I write, I'm a business adviser, so even if this triggers a line at my door as long as opening day at McDonald's in Moscow, you've paid your money and you're entitled to the secrets of the temple.

1. Business is business. Don't try to use a personal crisis as a lever to increase your income. It's unfair and it won't work. No matter how sincere the cluckings of concern you hear from across the table might sound, trotting out little Wanda's orthodontic predicament is going to generate resentment, not sympathy. I'd estimate that over half the people who have asked me for a raise have tied it to a personal emergency in their family. This is worse than a three-base error. The raise request has to equate to your stellar performance. If you have a personal crisis, there are a number of means available to deal with it, both inside and outside the company. We're talking business here. Don't try to switch signals from the Financial News Network to the Family Channel.

2. Know what you're worth. You can't negotiate anything unless you know the market. Don't think you can march in and shoot the lights out by asking for a raise that's out of line with what your company—and your industry—pays people for performing at a similar level. Unless you know what your contemporaries and your competitors are getting, how can you know what your pay scale should be? Snoop around as best you can. It can do more than help you win a raise, it can save your job. Asking to be lifted to an unrealistic salary level is to invite the boss to encourage you to get it somewhere else: "Well, Elmo, since I'm sure you wouldn't have asked for what you did just now unless you'd checked around and found out what you're truly worth, and since we can't possibly pay it, I can only wish you well getting it from whomever. We're sure going to miss you around here, old sport."

3. Don't go in with an attitude. Calmly make your deci-

sion before the meeting whether you're prepared to issue an ultimatum. If you are, then know you can't put it in reverse and back down if the answer is, "Goodbye and good luck." Smart negotiators know that a threat is *not* a sign of strength, it's a sign of weakness, an attempt to get something for nothing rather than a win-win scenario. If you have to threaten, that means you'd rather get what you're asking for than be forced to carry out your threat. Otherwise, why bother to make the threat at all? Why not simply undertake the threatened action? By threatening, you've put yourself in a box: Once you give the ultimatum, if the other side doesn't accept it, you're forced to back it up ... exactly what you've signaled you prefer not to do.

4. Do your homework. Failure to prepare for the fateful meeting is the number-one omission of the raise seeker. If the satchel you're carrying into the boss's office doesn't weigh at least three pounds, then you're probably not in a position to make a convincing case that you're ready for an upsizing in the era of downsizing. And, as I will never tire of reminding you, have your rationale for a raise in writing. Like what? Like this:

a) Letters from customers praising your worth.

b) Supervisor's notes, scribbles, oral comments (preserved in *your* notes promptly jotted down) patting you on the back.

c) Your own notes, dated, done at the time, recording services above and beyond the call of duty, such as filling in on different jobs, starting a company audio tape library, putting in a customer survey program—in short, anything that made or saved the company money or became company policy.

d) Your own notes again, now under the heading of "Teamwork." This time point out your role *in* the line of duty, and *on* team assignments.

e) Your progress in education and in training programs. If you've earned any certificates or diplomas, include copies. Nothing like a lot of fancy engraving and scrollwork to certify your growing skills and value.

f) Take your desk calendar over the last year, log in every hour of overtime or extra work you performed on the page displaying the date you performed it, flag each date with a Post-it note, total the numbers on a separate sheet, put a great big rubber band around the whole thing, and add that to the growing pile.

g) Document your trade association work, your industry work, and also your civic activities, but only those affiliations where the company has encouraged your participation.

This is the short list. You can add a few of your own.

5. Now that you've demonstrated what you've done for the company in the past, it's time to show your boss what you're going to do for the company in the future. You can't hit anything unless you take aim, so show your boss what your goals are for next year and how you are going to accomplish them. They should be specific. Measurable. In writing.

6. Timing is everything. That's why the folks who sell those easy payment engagement rings don't advertise on "Top Cops" or "Rescue 911." They hire bedroom-voiced announcers and run their commercials at 3:00 A.M. on mood music radio. Don't ask for a raise when you just blew the General Motors account or when the last two quarters were downers. You're no more immune from the economic cycle than your company is. Wait until you've just moved a mountain or two or until the sun is shining again, and then go for it.

7. After you've read the company's mood, read the boss's. Know what's going on inside the boss's head. If he's stressed out, or if the company is doing gangbusters,

but your department is lagging, cease and desist. Remember your youth. You didn't ask Pop for the car keys if he had had a bad day at the office.

8. Know what you're going to do if you get turned down. How will you handle a turndown or a counteroffer? Be prepared to be gracious. Ask what it would take to get that raise so that next time around you've made it easy for them to say yes.

That's it. It wasn't so tough, was it? These are just common sense rules, as easy as one, two, eight. Follow them and you will dramatically increase your odds of getting a raise.

69

THE ENEMY WITHIN

One of my favorite stories is about the architect who finally got his first big job. He decided to have a huge party to celebrate and went into a new neighborhood bar and restaurant to make arrangements. While he was there, he noticed a newspaper. The headline read: "Hard Times Coming." That did it. He changed his mind. No party. "Haven't you heard," he told the owner, "hard times are coming." He then called his wife. "You know that new dress you ordered for the party? Cancel it. Hard times coming."

The wife called the dressmaker and canceled the dress. Hard times coming. The dressmaker called the developer of the new building where she was going to open her big new space. Cancel the space. Hard times coming. The developer called the architect. Tenants are bailing out. I can't hire you after all. Hard times coming. Then, of course, the architect went back to the bar to drown his sorrows. He spotted the paper across the room. The headline seemed bigger than ever, "Hard Times Coming." He got up for a closer look. The paper lay wrinkled in a corner. It had been used by the owner to wrap his glassware and china. The architect looked at it more closely. His eyes finally moved from the headline to the date. The paper was twenty years old.

Every crisis we face is multiplied when we act out of fear. Fear is a self-fulfilling emotion. When we fear something, we empower it to become fearful. If we refuse to concede to our fear, there is nothing to fear. Franklin Delano Roosevelt said it better: "The only thing we have to fear is fear itself."

The essence of moral and political leadership lies in the ability to force us to face our fears and, by so doing, overcome them. That was FDR's great talent, and he used it to lead the nation out of the Depression and on to victory in World War II. His programs were modest by today's standards, but his inspirational qualities were huge.

Even the most talented are not immune from the curse of fear. When Johannes Brahms was only twenty years old, it was evident he was a musical genius of the first order. On a visit to his idol, Robert Schumann, the great composer was so impressed with Brahms's gifts, both as a composer and as a musician, that Schumann declared that he had met the "next Beethoven." That did it for Brahms. For twenty-three years, he was unable to complete his first symphony for fear of having his work compared—unfavorably—to that of the supreme musical figure of all time. "To write a symphony is no joke," said Brahms, as he agonized and the world waited. Finally, the "First" was introduced in 1876. Schumann's prophecy proved true. Brahms's First Symphony was hailed as "Beethoven's Tenth" and has remained so popular that even today it is among the pieces most often performed in the classical repertoire. With the First at last, Brahms was able to chill out a bit, and he then went on to produce three more well-regarded symphonies in the remaining twenty years of his life.

Fear is a disease that rots our will to succeed. Take away the fear of rejection and we'll make the calls, beat the pavement, get the training, and do what has to be done to find work.

Unfortunately, when it comes to finding a job, we don't get the same kind of help in overcoming our fears as we do when it comes to fighting a war.

It's a do-it-yourself proposition.

Books like this can help, but this book isn't going to be there for you when the interviewer says "no," or when the boss closes the door on a Friday afternoon and tells you it's all over. Then, it's what you've done to prepare for the situation, and what you've got inside you, that's going to get you back up on the horse.

In 1987, I ran my first marathon in New York. I trained exceptionally hard, but, of course, training and the real thing are two different animals.

Every first-time marathoner has only one objective: to finish the twenty-six-mile course. And no first-time marathoner can be certain he or she will finish. When you have never done something before, how can you be certain you'll ever be able to do it? You can't. You're afraid.

I imagine it's like giving birth to your first child. It helps to think that two billion women have done it before, but if *you* haven't, it's a trip into the twilight zone, and that can be scary.

The New York City marathon is loaded with color because there are so many contestants, so much hype and media coverage, and so many spectators. There are over a million and a half people lining the route, cheering on the runners.

As I plugged along, somewhere between mile twelve and thirteen, a lady with her Walkman decided to give me a little encouragement. She dashed into the street to tell me, "Did you hear? Ibraham Hussein just finished in two hours, eleven minutes!" Great. I'm not halfway through and some guy from Kenya has already finished. The race, so far as we were racing against each other, was over. What was left for the rest of us dudes? Lap money? What incentive was there to finish?

Only this. To prove to myself that I could do it. Don't ever let anyone, even someone trying to help you, destroy your belief in yourself. At that halfway point, I still believed that I could finish what I'd started.

If there's no one else around to lead you out of the wilderness, you have to tough it out and be your own cheerleader. I finished the race, and no one, including Hussein, won more than I did that day.

You can win, too. I know you can, because you cared enough about winning to get whatever help that I, a total stranger, can offer you. The fact you are trying is more important, more indicative of your character and determination, than the substance of the advice you'll find here.

I'm proud of you for trying and for asking for my help. Don't ever stop believing in yourself, and you'll win whatever race you're in.

70

TRAVEL BY COACH

Jack Kemp, the Secretary of Housing and Urban Development in the Bush administration, was an NFL quarterback with the Buffalo Bills before he got into politics. He tells the story of how his college coach at Occidental asked him into his office for a talk before the start of the season. "What he wanted me to know was that each year, there was one player, and one player only, that he was keeping his eye on because he saw that this one player had that special quality. One player who, if he lived up to his potential, would not only hold the team together, and bring it a championship, but who could also go on to greatness as a professional. He told me that this year, that

one player was me. He said that I was to keep this conversation in strictest confidence. No one, particularly no
one else on the team, was to know of this conversation,
because anyone I told this to would become very upset.
Of course, when I left the room that day, I was ready to
run through a brick wall for that guy," said Kemp. "And
that's exactly what I did all year long. And, of course, as I
found out later, he had had exactly the same little chat
with every other guy on the squad."

Nothing beats a great coach—in setting goals, in setting tougher goals, in keeping your vision broad, and in
helping you to endure the pain of the present—to enable
you to do what you must do now to achieve the goals you
have set for the future.

What makes these coaches great is not their ability to
con you; it's that their belief in you and in your latent talents is so strong that they know they can bring it out of
you if only they can make you believe in yourself.

The ironic thing is that they practice exactly the same
sort of hype on themselves as they do on others.

At the time of his death, George Allen, who had
coached professionally for the Washington Redskins and
the Los Angeles Rams, was the head coach for Long Beach
State, a Division I school whose football program was in a
shambles. Things were so bad that the season before Allen
took over as the head coach, the football team had lost
every single game on its schedule. The school didn't even
have a proper stadium, and there were rumors that the
administration was going to drop football altogether. It
didn't matter to Allen; he didn't take the job for the
money, and he saw no disgrace in coaching at any level.
Coaching was his life.

When he died in 1991, at the age of 72, the *Los Angeles
Times* said Allen left a note by the phone. It read:

1) win a championship

2) have everybody graduate

3) build a stadium

4) then take a tough job

George Allen set goals and took tough jobs his entire life. No setback, no artificial age barrier, no personal or professional obstacle could stop him. Only death could stop him, and even then, his influence was so strong and the lessons he taught were so ingrained in those who knew him that, according to the *Los Angeles Times* article, his funeral was diagramed by the staff of the Rolling Hills Covenant Church as carefully as Allen himself had diagramed a red-dog defensive blitz against the Dallas Cowboys.

I graduated in 1954 from the University of Minnesota and, as I've mentioned previously, while there I had played on the golf team coached by Les Bolstad. Thirty-eight years later, I still continue to keep in touch with him, because I'm so grateful for what he taught me, not only about the game of golf but about the game of life.

There's someone in your life like that: a coach, a teacher, a minister, a priest, a parent, a relative, a friend. Usually, there's more than one. Don't ever lose touch with these people. They believed in you then and they'll believe in you now. They'll help you get over the rough spots.

71

WHY LIFE IS LIKE BASEBALL

No matter what the circumstances, you always need a plan. When the Dodgers were playing the Mets in the '88 National League playoffs, Tommy Lasorda, the Dodger manager, was so sorely pressed for pitching he had to use his ace, Orel Hershiser, in relief only the day after he had started a game. Though Lasorda needed Hershiser just to get one final out to win the game, it was obvious the Dodgers' chances of winning would decrease with each pitch the exhausted Hershiser was forced to throw. As it turned out, Hershiser got his man.

"Tom, did you have a plan if he couldn't get that out?" Lasorda was asked after the game.

"Sure, I had a plan," said Lasorda. "A manager always

has to have a plan. My brothers were in the stands and if that guy had gotten a hit, they were going to shoot out the lights."

Stay focused, do not let yourself become distracted from your goals. "Jolly Cholly" Grimm managed the notoriously weak-hitting Chicago Cubs teams during the 1930s and '40s. One day he was approached by a scout who told him he had just witnessed the most phenomenal pitching performance he'd ever seen. "This kid didn't walk anyone or give up a single hit. No one even got a foul off him until the ninth inning. Should I sign him?"

"Hell, no," said Grimm. "Sign the guy who hit the foul ball. We need hitters."

Distinguish between what is important and what is unimportant. Don't forget what really matters in life. One of the small, quiet rituals of American life is the annual induction ceremony into the Baseball Hall of Fame. Other sports have their halls of fame, football, basketball, and hockey, but it's the baseball one that gets most of the attention, and deservedly so. The others are the *now* games. Baseball is the memory game. It is the game your father took you to.

So every summer, we have these paunchy, aging, one-time athletes trudging up to a microphone in a small town in upstate New York, wiping away a few tears, and trying to tell us what this game they played means to them and, in so doing, tell us what it means to us.

But for all their God-given athletic talent, they are common clay like the rest of us. Now they have been called upon, briefly, to be poets and philosophers. It's an unfamiliar role, but because they are, by definition, world-class at rising to the occasion, most of them are quite good at it.

Harmon Killebrew, a gentle giant who hit lots and lots of home runs, mounted the podium for his induction a few years ago. He talked about his childhood, the small western town where he'd grown up, the warm and loving family that had nurtured him. Every summer evening he and his brother and his dad would play catch in the back yard until they could no longer see the ball. His mother would grow hoarse trying to call her men into the house for dinner.

One evening, slightly exasperated, she tried a new tack. "Now you get in here. You're tearing up the grass," she called from the back door.

"We're not raising grass," her husband responded quietly. "We're raising boys."

Fathers and sons and mothers and daughters.

These are the memories that sustain us when the job grows too much to bear or is simply taken away from us.

We think we have become our jobs, but we haven't. We have become ourselves.

The experiences of our childhood are what give us our values. They give us the strength we need to cope.

This is a book about jobs, but no matter what happens, *a job is only a job*. It is just the grass under our feet. The nurturing and the growth and the preservation of *you as you* is what matters. That's the way the people who care about you have always seen it. Let them be there for you, even if it is just in memory, even as the daylight fades.

After all, it's only a game. Enjoy it while you can.

72

PAY DAY

For the majority of employees, the most dreaded words they ever hear are, "You're fired!" Not for salespeople. For them, it's "We're cutting your territory!" That's worse than being fired. You're being punished for being successful. You've sweated and scratched for years for every sale, finally made it happen, and then management tells you they've decided to turn over a big chunk of your turf to someone they can get for less money than they've been paying you.

It's as if you were a pioneer, went out and homesteaded a big section of virgin land, cleared it, plowed it, planted it, finally brought in a decent crop, and then were told you had to either give up half of it or move on down the road.

At least when you're fired, the cord has been cut. For better or for worse, you're free, free to sink or swim, to succeed or fail, to parlay your skills into a better paying position or roll over and play dead.

The territorial imperative leaves you in limbo. You're forced to make the decision yourself; accept less pay or take the plunge.

Steve Nichols (and that's his real name) took the plunge. From the very start of his career with the company, his sales chart had been climbing a steep north slope. He had built a solid reputation and an ever-expanding customer base representing an industrial supplies firm in Duluth. It may not sound glamorous; selling industrial supplies to miners and shippers doesn't exactly carry the same panache as slipping Roseanne Arnold into a Mercedes that matches the color of her eyes. But to a true salesperson, there's the same buzz no matter what you're selling, no matter where you're selling it, whenever the customer says the magic words, "You've got the order!"

And so it was, a typical American story, good sales rep, good company, sell, sell, sell for another twenty-five years until you collect the gold watch. Then after thirteen years with the company, came the ultimatum. And though most people would go with the flow, no matter how slow, Stevo said "no."

Now comes the hard part.

For the next six months, Steve put the same effort, actually *twice* the effort, that he had put into building his business into finding a job.

All of it uphill, into the wind, kicking, biting, clawing, and it produced exactly zip.

One day there was a slight ray of hope. He came

across an ad in the newspaper that looked as though it had his name written all over it. Steve zeroed in on his resume, making sure it was not one-size-fits-all and fine-tuned it until it purred. Seven days later, the phone rang. Having long since exhausted the slim job prospects in the area, Steve was out of town chasing down a lead. The caller told his wife, Andrea, that he wanted Steve to come in for an interview, casually adding this comforting news, "Oh, yes, you might want to tell Steve that there have been over three hundred applicants for the position."

Despite the odds, Steve threw himself into the effort the way he always did before making a sales call: total immersion. Olympic hopefuls could take lessons in commitment from Steve Nichols. He sent an overnight letter to the interviewer telling him how excited he was about the upcoming interview.

Steve's preparation was flawless. He had already gone to a bookstore and was current on all the latest job hunting techniques. He went to the library for industry background, called the company for information, contacted employees, customers, vendors, analyzed catalogs, did mock interviews, and within a week, was confident he had lapped the field of possible competitors.

When the interview itself came, he was comfortable, relaxed and effective because he had been over the course so many times. He also learned a valuable piece of information: of the three hundred applicants, only fifteen were being interviewed. The first cut had been a big one.

Not surprisingly, Steve made the second cut as well. He got a call back. "We would like you to come in for more interviews at our Kentucky home office plant."

Now it was back to the practice pit again. More data needed, more research, this time including the town he was traveling to on the edge of Cincinnati.

By the time he got there for this second round of interviews, he knew more about the lay of the land than if he had been assigned to jump in and capture the company headquarters with a division of paratroopers. With the help of friends, he had located friends of friends who lived there, arrived early and filled in the blanks of the information his other research hadn't uncovered.

He made the next cut, too.

Now it was time for the final elimination.

He was told there were two candidates left.

After he got back home, they called him from Kentucky. Would he agree to a phone interview with the company's industrial psychologist? Sure.

Then written tests. Then more telephone interviews. Then more written tests.

On August 8th, 1992, Steve Nichols got the call.

"We would like to offer you the position you've applied for. Will you accept?"

"Yes, Sir!"

A few minutes later *my* phone rang.

"I got the job! I got the job! It works! It really works!"

The caller did not give his name. He didn't have to. Throughout this entire eight and a half month period, Steve Nichols and I had been in constant contact. He had read my previous two books and came in to see me to ask my advice. As one thing in his life led to another, we sat down on half a dozen occasions and spoke on the phone many, many times. Together we plotted strategy, traveled the hills and valleys, rejoiced over the ups, commiserated over the inevitable downs, and finally reached the end of the journey.

If phone-a-vision were in place now, they couldn't have built a screen big enough to show our smiles. His was a mile wide. Mine was wider.

"That's … just … great!" I exclaimed.

One person. Just one person. You never know when

you write these things if you're going to help even a single human being. And when you do, when you know you have actually made a difference, it's the most wonderful feeling you can ever have. I know that's true, because I just experienced it. By believing in me, he made me believe in myself.

Steve Nichols got the job, but I got something more. What I did for Steve Nichols could never match what he did for me.

73

HOW TO TELL WHEN YOU'RE RICH

When I was a kid, watermelon was a great delicacy. The cost of shipping fruit and produce from a place like California to Minnesota, where I grew up, was prohibitive. With our short northern growing season, summer fruits like watermelon were just that: unknown except for a month or two in the summertime when they were home-grown.

Like every good newspaperman, my father, the local Associated Press man, knew everybody in town. One of his buddies was Bernie, who had once played football in the Big Ten, and after that fleeting moment of fame, wound up as a prosperous fruit and vegetable wholesaler, operating out of the warehouse district in St. Paul.

Every year, deep into the blistering Midwest summer, when the first watermelons would start to roll in, my dad would get a call from Bernie. We'd go down to his warehouse and take up our positions. We'd sit on the edge of the dock, feet dangling, trying to lean over far enough to minimize the volume of watermelon juice we were about to spill on ourselves.

Bernie would take his machete, crack our first watermelon of the season, and hand us both a big piece and sit down next to us. Then we'd bury our faces in watermelon, eating only the heart ... the reddest, juiciest, firmest, seed free-est, most perfect part ... and throw the rest away.

My father never made a lot of money. We were raised to be members of the clean plate club and all that. Bernie was my father's idea of a rich man. And I always thought it was because he'd been such a success in business. It was years before I realized that what my father admired about Bernie's wealth was less its substance than its application. Bernie knew how to stop work in the middle of the day, get together with his friends, and eat the heart of the watermelon. And throw the rest away.

Being rich isn't just about money. Being rich is a state of mind. Some of us, no matter how much money we have, will never have enough, never be free enough to eat only the heart of the watermelon and say: "The hell with the rest. I don't need to suck it dry. I can afford to let it go. I've had the best part." Some people will never be rich enough to do that. Some people are rich without ever being more than a paycheck ahead of the game.

Fired, hired. Stuck in a job rut or scurrying up the success ladder. If you don't take time to dangle your feet over the dock and chomp into life's small pleasures, you're letting your career overwhelm your life.

For many years, I forgot that lesson I'd learned as a kid

on the warehouse loading dock. Too busy, I guess. Making money. All the money I could make. Raising a family. Playing a role in the community. As big a role as I could play. The whole nine yards. Well, I've relearned it. And I hope I have a little time left to put the knowledge to use. To enjoy what I have. To find enjoyment in the accomplishments of others. My family. My friends. To take pleasure in the day and not worry too much about tomorrow. That's the heart of the watermelon. I finally learned to throw the rest away again.

Now I'm finally rich.

KURT EINSTEIN'S 20 MOST REVEALING INTERVIEWING QUESTIONS AND ANSWERS

There are always more job candidates than there are jobs, so it's a lot easier to eliminate unsuitable candidates than to attempt to find the one perfect applicant. An interview is a kind of ritual duel, where the interviewer is continually thrusting and probing for information, hoping to draw blood, while the candidate is parrying, trying to stay alive. Every question is a potential trap, where saying either too much or too little can be fatal. Kurt Einstein's comments apply to the interviewer. Mine are advice for the interviewee.

---

1. QUESTION: What have you been criticized for during the last four years?

   ANSWER:

   Kurt Einstein: It's interesting to know what the candidate would admit to.

   Harvey Mackay: This question is a real test of your negotiating skills—that is, negotiating as in, "He negotiated the rapids without tipping over in his canoe and drowning." You must provide something that isn't so serious as to be disqualifying yet not so trivial as to appear that you're either concealing your flaws or taking the question too lightly. I'd give high marks to a candidate who came up with something like, "I offered some ideas that I felt were constructive, but I was told not to rock the boat"; or, "I usually finished my assignments more quickly than my peers and some of them resented it"; or "I'd take courses at night when everyone else was in the bowling league and I was told I was an oddball." Don't try these, though, unless you can back it up, because the inevitable follow-up request is: "Okay, wise guy, prove it." I have to admit that others, like the *National Business Employment Weekly,* are quite critical of the "Little Ms./Mr. Perfect" answer, like "I'm a workaholic," or "I'm a stickler for detail."

The answers I give here don't go quite that far, but they are border-line. They would advise shifting the emphasis off yourself with something like "I'm learning to be more tolerant of the mistakes of others." If you ask me, that's a distinction without a difference. I still think we've got the right approach.

2. QUESTION: Did you agree or disagree and why?

   ANSWER: KE: If he agreed with some ... you've identified an area of weakness; if he disagreed with all ... an inflexible candidate, hard to manage.

   HM: Agreeing with some of the criticism seems to me to be a lot better answer than agreeing with none of it or all of it. Only a megalomaniac thinks he or she is always right and only a schnook thinks he or she is always wrong.

3. QUESTION: Where would you like to be in 3–5 years?

   ANSWER: KE: Observe whether candidate plans ahead and sets goals.

   HM: Bag this answer: "I'd like your job." It's been overworked more than "Officer, I didn't know I was speeding."

3a. QUESTION: And how do you expect to get there?

ANSWER: KE: This will indicate whether the previous answer was truthful or pro-
grammed. Ask them to explain in
detail.

                HM: Get beyond the obvious—i.e., "hard
work," or "I plan to take lots of
courses." Be clear and specific as to
how to meet the requirements and
responsibilities and obtain the skills
to execute your career plan. There's
a study you should be aware of:
Over a quarter of a century ago, an
Ivy League University interviewed a
class of graduating seniors and
asked them if they had clear, specific career goals. Three percent said
yes; 97 percent said no. They interviewed the same group again after
twenty-five years. The 3 percent
with the goals had 97 percent of the
wealth. Two conclusions are obvious: 1) set goals, stay focused,
adjust your plan to meet changing
conditions; 2) your interviewer is
probably aware of the study.

4.   QUESTION: What would you like to change in
this job to make it ideal?

    ANSWER: KE: Why would he want to change it?

                HM: "I don't think it should be changed.
I do think it has to be mastered, and
that's an exciting and challenging
opportunity. Obviously, at some
point in my career, I'd hope to be

able to handle even more responsibility."

4a. QUESTION: How would you describe the most and least ideal boss you could choose?

ANSWER: KE: Indicates personality preferences. Indicates "would he or she fit with future boss."

HM: Cute, isn't it? Particularly, since you probably don't have a clue at this time what your potential boss is like. You should finesse this one a bit: "I've worked with hard-driving, demanding bosses, and I've worked with bosses who've had such a light touch on the throttle, I've barely had any real supervision or direction. I can adapt to any style." And then, move in for the kill: "But, if you really pinned me down, I'd say it would be someone who gave me enough direction so I had a specific idea of what was expected of me and had enough restraint to let me do my thing without hovering over me every step of the way."

5. QUESTION: What activities in your position do you enjoy most?

ANSWER: KE: Indirect way of ascertaining areas of weakness.

HM: If you have strong feelings about what you like best, you're also revealing the opposite … what you like least. What are good things to like least? Well, for one, "bad morale." So, you might say, "Being part of a winning team." Who wants to be part of a losing one?

6. QUESTION: How would you describe yourself with three adjectives?

ANSWER: KE: Delve for three *negative* adjectives.

HM: Here's another loaded gun. Obviously, no negative adjectives need apply, but even positive ones can have negative implications if they're grouped in a way that suggests a weakness. For instance, "intelligent, efficient, reliable." All great attributes, but when grouped together suggest an absence of human qualities. Is this person arrogant and aloof? Does he or she get along with people? The grouping "friendly, cooperative, a team player" suggests fine personal qualities but a possible weak performer. Best to *combine* a few virtues to suggest strengths in both ability and personality, such as "goal-oriented, likeable, successful."

6a. QUESTION: How would your subordinates describe you with three adjectives?

ANSWER: KE: What are the differences? Is the candidate sensitive to how other people see him or her?

HM: In my opinion, the correct response is to give the same answer you gave for number 6, and then smile sweetly and wait for the next question.

7. QUESTION: Do you think you praise enough?

   ANSWER: KE: Secure people have less problems giving praise than insecure people. Psychological attitude toward praise indicates interest and ability to motivate. Development of self-esteem.

   HM: "I love to get it, so I love to give it."

8. QUESTION: What would you do if you detected a peer falsifying expense records?

   ANSWER: KE: Indicates passive or active approach. Common answers: a) It's not my business, b) Report it, c) Give warning. Gives indication as to morality, honesty, and ethics.

   HM: In my opinion, the first answer is so bad I'd be tempted to stop the interview right there and send the candidate home. If you can't even be trusted to protect the company's interests against dishonesty, why should they hire you? This isn't swiping cookies out of your third-grade classmate's lunch pail. This is the real world. So get real. The third answer is acceptable, barely. It finesses the conflict between being a squealer and letting someone rip off your employer. Understandable, but still weak. Two is best. There's a fourth approach, another finesse, which has the virtue of being a bit more proactive than the third answer: Confront culprits point-blank and try to persuade them to change the erroneous report *without* issuing a specific threat as to what your conduct will be if they don't.

9. QUESTION: What would you do if the company you just joined gave you three thousand dollars to spend during the first year in any way you felt appropriate?

ANSWER: KE: May reveal areas of weakness if job related, or poor attitude if not job related. Important question is *Why?*

HM: The obvious answer is the right one: a job-related use, such as taking courses. But you must be prepared for the inevitable follow-up question, "Why?" because it is intended to probe for evidence of weakness, such as your lack of adequate experience or training for the position you're seeking. So be sure that if you answer "education," the course work you describe is more advanced than that required for the immediate job.

10. QUESTION: If you had a choice, would you

rather draw up plans or implement them?

ANSWER: KE: Draw up: Has tendency to think, innovate, conceptualize, theorize, risk taker. Implement: has tendency to be a doer, follower (can be positive or negative).

HM: Don't choose "implement" unless the major piece of equipment used in the job you are applying for is a broom.

11. QUESTION: State three situations in which you did not succeed. *Why?*

ANSWER: KE: Does he or she admit to any? Blame others? Is the candidate self-assured? Has he or she learned from it, and, if so, what?

HM: Kurt's notes spell out the elements of a winning answer. First, admit to having failed at something. In my opinion, one example is too few: It suggests rigidity, a willingness to make only the barest, most grudging admission of the possibility of error. Three examples are too many. That response suggests that had the questioner asked for more than three, hey, no problem, you would have been able to come up with whatever number of additional failures were needed. Pick *two*—i.e., an attempt to get an A+ that netted only an A. Or a second-place finish in whatever. Hardly "real" failures, but admitting to having caused several total disasters is hardly in your best interests. Next, obviously, you don't "blame others" for your own failures. And, of course you are "self-assured." Finally, what "you've learned" is to try harder next time, be better prepared, not to let defeat get you down or become a habit, and that succeeding is a lot better than failing.

12. QUESTION: When you fire somebody, what would be your key objective? Why?

ANSWER: KE: Look for: "It was deserved." "It's beyond my control." "Protect myself legally." "Keep company image clean." "Get inside scoop/grapevine." Or: Considers employee's feeling, shows sympathy.

HM: "I felt I was acting in the best interests of both the company and the employee in question." Follow-up question: "Why?" Follow-up answer: "From the company's point of view, the employee's performance did not meet our standards and expectations. Despite repeated attempts to help the employee improve, performance was still not adequate."

13. QUESTION: What need do you expect to satisfy by accepting this position?

ANSWER: KE: This gives candidates the chance to

identify their most important career needs.

HM: Your needs better track the company's needs pretty closely, or what you're still going to be needing is a job. I would lean toward answers that stress the satisfaction of setting goals, achieving them, and setting new goals. Companies see employees the way track and field fans see high jumpers. Every time the athlete clears the bar, they want to set it a little higher for the next jump.

14. QUESTION: What would you like to change in this job to make it ideal?

ANSWER: KE: How does the candidate respond when an authority figure makes an error?

HM: Here's the trick question of all time: question 4 is repeated here as question 14. Did you notice? If so, now what? Is this some kind of weird psychological test? A memory game? Do you pretend it didn't happen? Is the interviewer trying to see if you change your answer? Do you correct him or her? Are you made noticeably nervous by the interviewer's "error"? Kurt doesn't give us a clue as to what the "right" response is, but my guess is that the only really wrong one is to overreact and make a big deal out of it. I'd answer in totally deadpan fashion: "I think this may have come up earlier, and as I recall, I said I felt no need to change the job itself; the need was to master the job as it is and then, if the opportunity arose, to assume even greater responsibilities at some later point."

15. QUESTION: We all fib occasionally. Would you say something that is not entirely true? Give me three examples when you did.

ANSWER: KE: Discuss: Significant, insignificant, borderline lies.

HM: A tougher version of question 1. Again, this is to test your ability to walk the line between the answer that is too revealing and the answer that is too concealing. But there's really a lot more happening here than meets the eye. Like question 14, this one is designed to measure how forthright and honest you are in your reactions to an authority figure. This time the authority figure has not just made an inadvertent "error," he or she has issued a pronunciamento, a moral judgment set forth as a statement of fact. He or she has said that everyone lies, and everyone includes you, so the premise on which the question is based is: *You lie.* All beautifully contained and concealed in this perfectly innocent-sounding, perfectly conventional, perfectly legal, plain-vanilla interview question. What's happening here is you're being tested not only on whether you fib but whether you will allow a perfect stranger to say that you do, when the person saying it can have a considerable impact on your future. Am I reading too much into this? Perhaps. Most of us do, in fact, fib. But remember, this test isn't designed to provide employment for candidates who most nearly correspond to the norm. It's designed to weed out average applicants and locate exceptional ones. I don't see anything the matter with challenging the we-all-lie premise. I'd answer as follows: "Oh, I don't think everyone lies, or, as you say, fibs. In my life, I've known people I believe never to have lied. So I have to tell you, I don't think your premise is correct. I cannot say I have met that standard myself and have never lied. I know I have. I will say, though, that when I have lied, I've tried to confine it to social situations. I'm afraid not every baby I've seen is movie-star material, and not every meal where I've been a guest has been worth four stars in the Michelin Guide."

16. QUESTION: What benefits can be expected from threatening an employee to do better?

ANSWER: KE: If answer is other than *none*, probe further for candidate management and motivation style.

HM: Threatening employees is usually not an attempt to improve performance. It's a calculated prelude to discharge. The threat is used in hopes of thwarting subsequent legal action ... "We warned him or her, so the firing shouldn't have come as a surprise." No one is fooled. The hope is that the employee will get the message and move on before the discharge takes place. And *that* is the only benefit of threatening.

16a. QUESTION: When would you do that?

ANSWER: KE: Ask for examples.

HM: Threats are as common in business as coffee breaks. Employers threaten employees. Unions threaten management. Management threatens unions. For instance, a customer threatens a supplier with replacement if punctuality doesn't improve. The customer knows how inconvenient it would be to commit the time, money, and effort to find a new supplier and, even then, not know if the new supplier would be any freer from defect than the old.

By threatening, the customer hopes to achieve the company's goal without effort. Thus, a threat is very often a sign of weakness rather than of strength. Why hesitate to take the action announced if you're willing and able to act immediately to achieve your goal?

17. QUESTION: If you encountered serious difficulties on this job, what would they be?

ANSWER: KE: Reveals candidate's area of weakness or fear.

HM: By now you should be able to ace this kind of probe. What you're concerned about, of course, is not failure but success. You anticipate no difficulties but would hope to work in an environment that values teamwork, rewards initiative, provides opportunities for advancement, achieves its goals, and is a congenial place to work.

18. QUESTION: What are three things you are afraid to find in this job?

ANSWER: KE: Explores candidate's *fears* (realistic or not).

HM: Another attempt to get you to spout negatives and reveal yourself as a bundle of psychoses. Since you fear nothing, you give the time-honored positive response. Your only concerns are that you have the opportunity to excel, and since your research has led you to believe this is the kind of place you can do it in, well, it's not a concern at all.

19. QUESTION: We all have negative areas we would like to improve. Do you agree? If you do, could you give me three areas in which you would like to improve?

ANSWER: KE: Weakness ... understanding of one-self.

HM: Another "we-all"er but this time worded in such a way that you're given the *option* of agreeing or not. So, now you can agree. Again, I'd stick with providing two instead of the requested three, on the theory that giving only one shows arrogance and inflexibility and three is a classic display of wimpiness in going along with whatever the authority figure demands. And again, I'd try to turn the question around so you can give yourself the opportunity to play to your strengths and not to your weaknesses. Thus, you want to continue to grow professionally. While you are certain you have the tools necessary to perform the job in question, no one can have too much education or preparation, and you're going to continue to take self-improvement courses, both those that provide professional training and those that are designed to help upgrade personal and inter-personal skills. Secondly, you never seem to have enough time to per-form service work on behalf of others, and there are various volunteer organizations you're interested in, such as Boy Scouts, Girl Scouts, and so on.

20. QUESTION: How do you motivate people?

    ANSWER: KE: a) Threat, b) fear, c) example.

             HM: I've already indicated why I believe threats are overrated and misunder-stood. Fear works. As you read here earlier, Bob Knight, the Indiana Uni-versity basketball coach, is a master at goading players into performing. But what motivates a nineteen-year-old college sophomore to excel in athletics over a brief, intense time span as part of a team, all of whose members have been equally abused by "Coach," won't work in just any setting. Where the personnel are mature, experienced, and profes-sional they will not regard mistreat-ment and claims of absolute author-ity as a source of inspiration. One of the most powerful motivators is "peer pressure." That's what the armed forces use to motivate soldiers. What makes an eighteen-year-old kid risk his life in combat? It sure isn't because he thinks his second lieutenant is such a prince. It's because his buddies, the guys he's bivouacked with since boot camp, will think he's a coward if he doesn't go with the flow. But peer pressure, despite its powerful impact as a motivator, is, like the other motivators, imposed from without, which means the values expressed are someone else's. It tends to work best on young people, because their personal set of values is not yet fully formed, and they are more easily influenced by others. I think the best motivator, the one that is most likely to stick with you, even for a lifetime, is the one that comes from within, the voice *inside* you that tells you to show 'em your stuff. If you're looking for a one-word description of a truly motivated person, I'd say "self-starter." Sure, the spark that lit that fire had to come from somewhere. It can be the product of your home environment, your religious upbringing, your drive to achieve success. But wherever that spark comes from, once it becomes part of *you,* what *you* believe, then external forces are merely tempo-

		rary, coming and going with the people who are imposing them.
EXTRA:		When do you think you have arrived? (definition of success).
ANSWER:	KE:	a) When I can collect Social Security, b) When I am president of the company, c) When I have your job, d) I will never arrive … neurotic need, constantly chafing at the bit. Explain "Compulsive Achievers." Difference between "wanting" and "having" to succeed.
	HM:	My definition is when you're rich enough to eat the heart of the watermelon and throw the rest away.

THE MACKAY SWEET SIXTEEN

If you want to hit the ground running, read and answer these sixteen questions ... you can't be *over-prepared*.

1. Describe your ideal job—the position you would most like to have. (Include title, responsibilities, who you would report to, who would report to you.)

2. Describe your ideal company (size industry, culture, location, structure).

3. Where do you want to be in your career in three to five years?

4. What do you want your next job to do for you that your last job didn't do?

5. What kinds of growth should a new job offer (promotions, training, challenges)?

6. What skills will you be able to add to your resume while you have this job?

7. Why should a company want to hire you? (What is special about you as a job candidate?)

8. What personal and professional accomplishments are you the most proud of?

9. What do you least want to be asked in an interview—the questions you dread the most?

10. How will you handle the tough questions?

11. What compensation, including salary and benefits, do you want to earn and can you legitimately ask for?

12. What are the most important benefits other than salary that would prompt you to go to work for a new company?

13. What tools and resources can you draw on to help you through your job transition?

14. What can you say in an interview that would really set you apart from other candidates for your ideal position?

15. What could your current employer do for you that would prevent you from looking for another job in the first place? (Have you asked?)

16. How will you know when you have become a success?

APPENDIX C

HOW TO SAVE YOUR OWN LIFE

My experience with cancer taught me an unforgettable lesson. I have told you in every way I know how that you've got to know your customer. But it won't matter how well you take care of your customer if you don't take care of yourself.

For you men fifty years old and up, this information can save your life! I discuss it in every speech I give, and after six months of market-testing, four people have already called me to say they're alive because they took the advice you're about to read.

Prostate cancer has been the number two killer in men since time immemorial. Each year 34,000 American males die from it. Though zillions of dollars have gone into cancer research, the death ratio from prostate cancer hasn't budged a quarter of 1 percent over the years. The female counterpart, breast cancer, is similar in its deadly effects if it's untreated, but women are incredibly more knowledgeable and proactive than men in dealing with "their" disease. That also explains why women live, on the average, seven years longer than men. It's not necessarily genetic.

The male tendency to avoid medical attention isn't a DNA-encoded gender signal. It's a cultural anomaly. Maybe pregnancy accustoms women to the indignities of being poked and prodded in private places by doctors. Maybe we hunter/gatherers think we have to go nonstop till we drop or there won't be enough food on the table. Whatever the reason, women log a total of a hundred million more doctor's visits annually, while we crawl back into our caves to macho it out.

Heredity plays a major role in both diseases. Because my father had prostate cancer, I was in a higher risk category, and because I'm a nut for staying in step with the music, I've always been alert to any new developments in this area.

There hasn't been much to report.

Until now.

Three years ago a breakthrough occurred. A blood test called the PSA (Prostate Specific Antigen) broke the medical sound barrier for early detection of prostate cancer. Draw some blood. Send it out to the lab and, within hours, you know if you're in the danger zone.

Thanks to that simple blood test, I'm not only still here, but by the time you read this, I will have already finished my fourth New York Marathon. And that gives me something new to nag you about. On behalf of your friends and family I've been self-appointed to officially inform you that you have no more excuses for not seeing the doctor and getting checked out. Now. Early. Painlessly.

What if you test positive and further testing does indeed show a malignancy? Your choices will probably be radiation or surgical removal. In my case, I had the surgery, but I walked five miles just nine days after surgery and got back into my five- to seven-mile running groove in six weeks. And I'm playing tournament tennis again. In short, I've never felt better mentally and physically. Sure, having surgery is not exactly fun and games, but you can take any amount of pain, *as long as you know it's going to end*. Ask any woman who's ever had a baby. We've all used that mental trick from the time we watched the clock in school ticking off the minutes until recess, the days until the weekend, the weeks until summer vacation. My father got me through my tonsillectomy with his version: "I'd get in the ring with Joe Louis for three rounds. I'd just think about the fourth round."

Surgery is tough, but you'll get through it and then you'll get over it. The alternative, denial, puts you and your loved ones in a hell of a lot tougher position. Temporary pain is still pain, but it's still temporary, too.

One last word on the subject: It makes me very sad and very angry to tell you that your health plan may not cover the PSA test. It could cost you thirty to forty dollars out of your own pocket. It's worth it. It could turn out to be the best investment you've ever made.

No more excuses.

It's just like Arnold.

The boss called him into the office to see if he had any explanation for his miserable job performance. "I've gone over your supervisors' reports, and I think you ought to be aware of some of the concerns that have been expressed. For instance, on your first assignment, on the assembly line, the foreman writes, 'Arnold does not seem to have a grasp of the need for arriving at work on time.' Then you went to the shipping department, and the manager there says, 'We have had a record number of returns this month, due to Arnold's habit of mislabeling our deliveries.' And, here's one from your current department head, in marketing: 'We had to have a recall of all our point of purchase posters when we discovered Arnold had misspelled the name of the company.'

"That's quite a record. Three separate jobs and three disasters. What I really ought to do is fire you. What do you have to say to that?"

"The same thing I said before. I'll try to do better next time, Dad."

Let's not be too hard on Arnold, though. Perhaps he was a student of George Bernard Shaw, who wrote, "I dread success. To have succeeded is to have finished one's business on earth, like the male spider, who is killed by the female the moment he has succeeded in courtship. I like a state of continual becoming, where the goal is in front, and not behind."

The ability to keep learning, to keep yourself in a state of continual becoming, is what this book is all about. It's a gift that can help keep your job, find your future, or save your life.

NOTES

PAGE

12. Monthly Labor Review 1987, Bureau of Labor Statistics, Occupational Projections and Training Data Institute.

14. "White Collar, Blue Collar: Jobs Are Vanishing," *Barron's,* May 11, 1992, p. 9.

14. "Many Workers Facing First Interview In Years," *Naples Daily News,* March 22, 1992, p. 54G.

15. *Barron's,* May 11, 1992, p. 22.

19. "The Answers to Your Questions About Suction Cups," *Naples Daily News,* March 15, 1992, p. 63G.

19–20. "Upscale Off-Price Stores Do Very Well For

Retailer", *Naples Daily News,* March 15, 1992, p. 76G.

20. *New York Times,* May 10, 1992, p. 11.

21. "Is America on the Way Down?," *Commentary,* May 1992.

22. *Commentary,* May 1992, p. 21.

22. *Commentary,* May 1992, p. 27.

23. *Occupational Outlook Handbook,* 1990–91, U.S. Bureau of Labor Statistics, p. 9.

23. *Barron's,* May 11, 1992, p. 24.

24. "Retirement at 65 was first proposed by the 19th century German statesman Otto von Bismarck. It took root in the U.S. during Franklin Delano Roosevelt's New Deal." "The Graying Yuppie," *New York Magazine,* March 9, 1992, p. 36. "45 percent of respondents (to a U.S. News poll of 1200 adults conducted by Princeton Research Associates May 3–7, either are or expect to be working after age 65." "Still Working," *U.S. News & World Report,* May 25, 1992, p. 80.

24. "Labor Letter," *Wall Street Journal,* May 12, 1992, p. 1.

26. "Successful Executives Quitting to Begin New Businesses," *Miami Herald,* May 29, 1992, p. 11.

26–27. "Eastern Experience Put to Work by Fort Lauderdale Entrepreneur," *Miami Herald,* March 23, 1992, p. 13.

27. "After the Pay Revolution, Job Titles Won't Matter," *New York Times,* May 17, 1992, p. C5.

28. "More than 70% of all new jobs are being created by companies with fewer than 500 employees, reports the U.S. Small Business Administration." "Reaching for the Best Opportunity," "Managing Your Career" (supplement), *National Business Employment Weekly,* Spring 1992, p. 4.

32. Connelly, Thomas, editor, *Almanac of American Presidents,* Facts on File, New York, 1991.

34. *The World Almanac and Book of Facts,* 1992, p. 425.

43. *Wall Street Journal,* April 27, 1992.

45. "When Products Are Tied to Causes," *New York Times,* April 18, 1992.

50–51. "A Litany of Euphemisms for 'You're Fired,'" *Executive Recruiter News,* November 1990, published in *Harper's,* March 1991.

51. *Sports Illustrated,* October 29, 1990, p. 76.

52. *New York Times,* March 26, 1979.

55. *The Speaker's Book of Quotations,* Fawcett Columbine, 1987, p. 209.

64. "Networking," in supplement titled "Managing Your Career, the College Edition of the National Business Employment Weekly," *National Business Employment Weekly,*" Spring 1992, p. 27.

77–78. *Skyway News,* week of April 14–20, 1992, p. 1.

79. Office of Records, University of Michigan, August 17, 1992.

83. Godfrey, Arthur, *Tell It to the King,* G. P. Putnam, 1988.

87. *Statistical Abstract of the U.S. 1991.*

90. "Are You a Job Snob?," "Managing Your Career, The College Edition of the National Business Employment Weekly," p. 10, *National Business Employment Weekly,*" Spring 1992.

90. Ibid.

92. *The Miami Herald,* May 1, 1992, p. 4C; *Naples Daily News,* March 22, 1992, p. 62G.

92–93. "Young People Don't Want to Become Toolmakers," *Naples Daily News,* March 22, 1992, p. 62G.

125. From William Safire's commencement address to Syracuse University's class of 1990 reprinted in

"slightly edited" form in the *Miami Herald,* May 27, 1990, p. 6G.

128. *World Almanac and Book of Facts,* 1992.

128. *The Forbes Scrapbook of Thoughts on the Business of Life,* Trimph, Chicago, 1992, p. 40.

193. *Forbes Magazine,* Sept. 17, 1979.

208. *Albany Times Union,* June 11, 1992, p. 1A.

264–265. Wright, Lawrence, "The Man from Texarkana," *New York Times Magazine,* June 28, 1992, p. 20.

323. "Should You Get Tested," *U.S. News & World Report,* May 4, 1992.

RECOMMENDED READING LIST

When Bad Things Happen to Good People, Rabbi Harold Kushner, 1989 Schocken

Zen and the Art of Motorcycle Maintenance: An Inquiry Into Values,, Robert Pirsig, 1974 Morrow

Thriving on Chaos, Thomas J. Peters, Knopf

Liberation Management: Necessary Disorganization for the Nano-Second Nineties, Tom Peters, 1992 Knopf

Power of Positive Thinking, Norman Vincent Peale, 1992 Fawcett

What Color is Your Parachute?: A Practical Manual for Job-Hunters & Career Changers, Richard B. Bolles, 1993 Ten Speed Press

The One Minute Manager, Kenneth Blanchard and Spencer Johnson, 1987 Berkley

The Psychology of Winning, Denis Waitley, 1984 Berkley

Success Magazine, Scott DeGarmo, editor-in-chief & publisher

Think and Grow Rich, Napoleon Hill, 1987 Fawcett

You Can Negotiate Anything, Herb Cohen, 1983 Bantam

Inc. magazine, George Gendron, editor-in-chief

Customers for Life, Carl Sewell & Paul B. Brown, 1991 Bantam Books

Think and Grow Rich: A Black Choice, Dennis Kimbro & Napoleon Hill, 1992 Fawcett

The Road Less Traveled, M. Scott Peck, 1988 Simon & Schuster

National Business Employment Weekly, newsletter

Small Decencies: Reflections & Meditations on Being Human at Work, John Cowan, 1992 HarperBusiness

The Addictive Organization: Why We Overwork, Cover Up, Pick up the Pieces, Please the Boss, and Perpetuate Sick Organizations, Anne Wilson Schaef and Diane Fassel, 1990 Harper SF

Working Ourselves to Death: The High Cost of Workaholism & the Rewards of Recovery, Diane Fassel, 1992 Harper SF

Do What You Love, the Money Will Follow: Discovering Your Right Livelihood, Marsha Sinetar, 1989 Dell

The Customer Comes Second: And Other Secrets, Hal Rosenbluth, 1992 Morrow

Believing in Myself: Meditations for Healing & Building Self-Esteem, Earnie Larsen and Carol Hegarty, 1991 Prentice-Hall

Calling It a Day, Robert Larranga, 1990 Harper SF

The 7 Habits of Highly Effective People, Stephen R. Covey, 1990 Simon & Schuster Trade

INDEX

I believe so strongly in successful networking that I've written a book about it. You can now order *The Harvey Mackay Rolodex Network Builder* by calling 1-800-374-6695 and I'll send it to you for $3.95. This is an $8.95 retail value.

If you have thoughts, comments, or ideas about this book, I'd love to hear from you. (Please, no requests for personal advice.) Write to me at the following address:

Harvey Mackay
Mackay Envelope Corporation
2100 Elm Street Southeast
Minneapolis, Minnesota 55414